What is OMA

Considering Rem Koolhaas and the Office for
Metropolitan Architecture

Considering Rem Koolhaas and the Office for
Metropolitan Architecture   NAi Publishers, Rotterdam

WHAT IS

Contents

Area   152

describes OMA's field of work, set against the background
of economic, societal and political changes between 1972 and 2003.
This field of work ranges, on the one hand, from Seattle to
Beijing and from Rotterdam to Porto, on the other hand it deals
with diverse forms of 'architecture': theoretical research, actual
building projects and media projects.

Preface

Traditional architecture criticism tends to conclude any study of an OMA proj-ect with either generic praise for the work's wit, its renewed attention to the city, its perceived reanimation of dormant social responsibilities, or its neo-modern avoidance of formal excess; or, trite condemnation for its neo-modern avoidance of formal excess, its cartoonishly reductive diagrams, or its cheap, even ugly, construction. Each of these judgements can be confirmed in one or another of OMA's projects, but none grasps why Koolhaas's architecture has today become the most debated and influential in the world.[1,2]

For quite some time now, it seems no debate on architecture and urban planning can take place without reference to the projects, the research or the pronouncements of Rem Koolhaas. Koolhaas and the Office for Metropolitan Architecture exert an extraordinarily far-reaching influence on contemporary international architecture. And yet it is clear that, beyond a circle of initiates, few realise the scope of OMA's work. This terse observa-tion on the position and significance of the work of Rem Koolhaas and OMA led to the formulation of this book. **What is OMA** is an attempt to analyse the multi-faceted work of Rem Koolhaas, to provide insights into its impor-tant themes and to elucidate the far-reaching significance of OMA.

To those who study the work of Rem Koolhaas in depth, it becomes abundantly clear that architecture can be more than simply the built envi-

1. The work's ascendancy to this position is confirmed by every standard indicator: the frequent appearance of the architect on short lists for high-profile projects, the popularity of publications about his work, the number and popularity of his personal appearances; the number of student imitations; the number of professional knock-offs, piracies, counterfeits and forgeries, the virulence of practitioners who explicitly position their own work against his, and the number of practitioners, both renowned and uncelebrated, who have openly declared a debt to him.
2. Jeffrey Kipnis, 'Recent Koolhaas', *El Croquis*, no. 79, 1996.

onment. Koolhaas described *S,M,L,XL,*[3] his most prestigious book so far, as a 'novel about architecture' and summed up its contents as an accumulation of 'essays, manifestoes, diaries, fairy tales, travelogues, a cycle of meditations on the contemporary city. . .' That book, and indeed all the projects and research that have followed *S,M,L,XL*, bear witness to the wide spectrum architecture encompasses and the many interfaces of architectural research.

Because OMA has such widespread impact, the office is also significant for other professions: philosophy, sociology, economics, literature, etcetera. In formulating this book, therefore, we primarily sought out authors outside the boundaries of architecture. Bart Verschaffel, Matthew Stadler, Bruce Sterling, Ian Buruma, Okwui Enwezor and Henk Hofland, as a philosopher, writers, a curator and a writer-journalist, respectively, elucidate OMA's work from their specific frames of reference and submit it to an often personal but always critical review. Aaron Betsky and Neil Leach supplement these approaches, from the angles of architecture criticism and architectural theory. Rather than describing individual projects, the various articles analyse their mutual cohesion and their relation to social and economic developments.

The framework of the book radically divides the multiplicity of attitudes adopted by the Office for Metropolitan Architecture into three sections: *Orbit, Method,* and *Area* successively compile OMA's importance, the methods applied and the different spheres of interest. *Orbit* includes reflections on the new meaning with which Koolhaas imbues the role of the architect, on Koolhaas's difficult relationship with the Netherlands and on the impact of Dutch tradition in OMA's work. In *Method*, the role of the visual and the aesthetic in OMA's work – in light of our contemporary culture – is analysed. Koolhaas's performance is compared to that of an ethnographer and an anthropologist on a quest for the remains of what we today call urbanism. Finally, the narrative in OMA's work is examined in relation to the concept of reality. The last chapter, **Area**, lays out the connection between theoretical discourse and building practice through a discussion of OMA's first buildings. The activities of the recently set-up AMO, OMA's alter ego, which specifically concentrates on the 'virtual', are also discussed.

Despite an amalgam of opinions, backgrounds, cultures and writing styles in the various authors, some projects and concepts come up in several texts and weave themselves as an invisible thread throughout the book. *Delirious New York*, 'The Generic City', 'Bigness' and 'The Berlin Wall as Architecture' prove permanent ingredients in discussing the work, regardless of the point of view. The implicit references to the numerous manifestoes, texts, books and essays illustrate the role and the significance of the written work of Rem Koolhaas. The fact that 'writing' occupies a special place within the architectural practice, with a role beyond that of registration, is also illustrated by this quote on the young Koolhaas, who, in the 1960s, as a journalist for the *Haagse Post* newspaper and as a member of the film collective '1, 2, 3, enz.' was influenced by, among others, the work of the Dutch author Willem Frederik Hermans: 'For Hermans, by the way, the only difference between "journalistic" and "literary" is that the journalist writes what the masses think while the novelist disputes what the masses think and brings to light what the masses do not dare to think. . . . In that sense Koolhaas is more a novelist than a journalist.'[4]

The novelist in Koolhaas keeps constructing a startling scenario to grasp the reality that surrounds him, to interpret it and cope with it. Obviously this aspect is one of the unique qualities of OMA's work and elevates it above the generally accepted interpretation of architecture as the 'craft of building'.

Véronique Patteeuw
editor, NAi Publishers

3. Rem Koolhaas, *S,M,L,XL*, New York/Rotterdam, 1995.
4. Bart Lootsma, 'Now switch off the sound and reverse the film ...', *Hunch* 1, 1999.

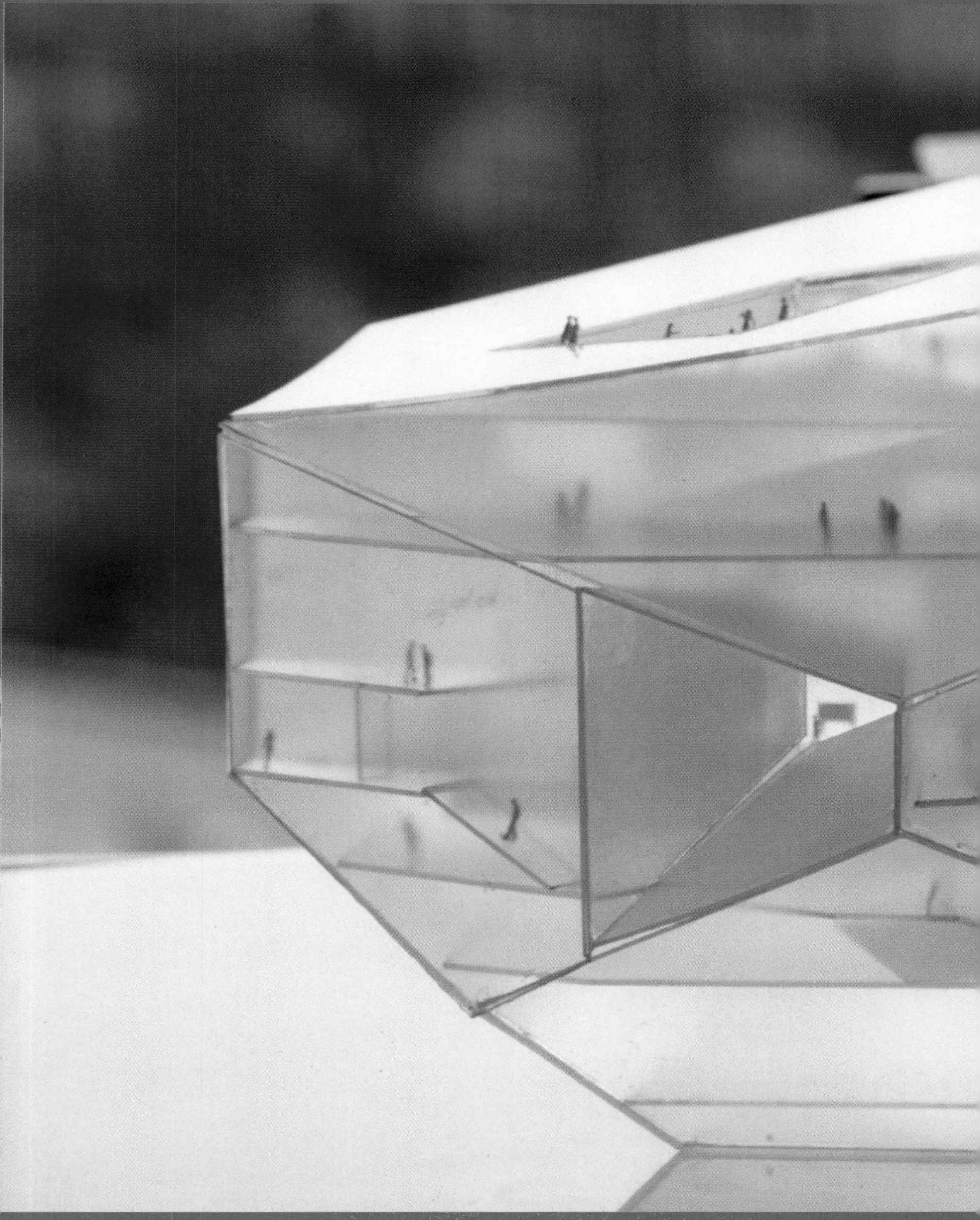

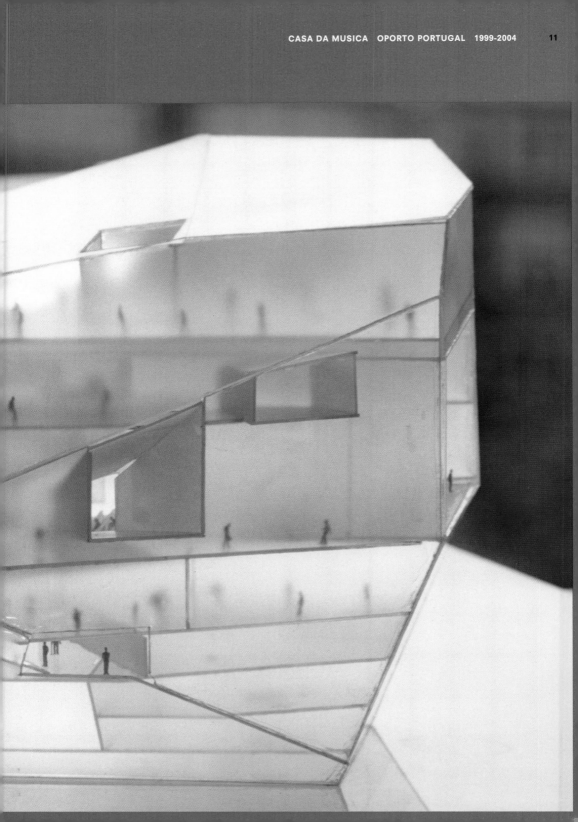

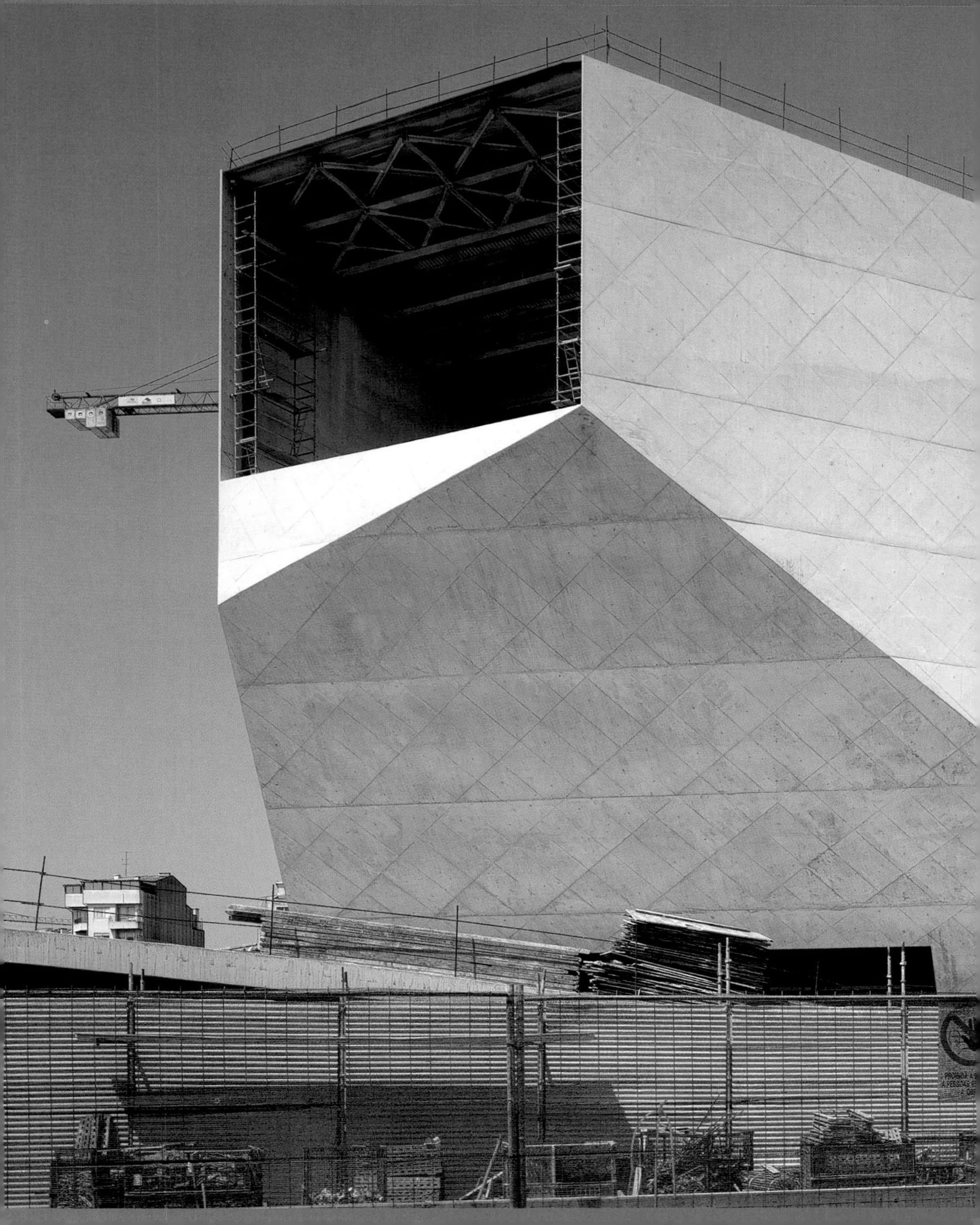

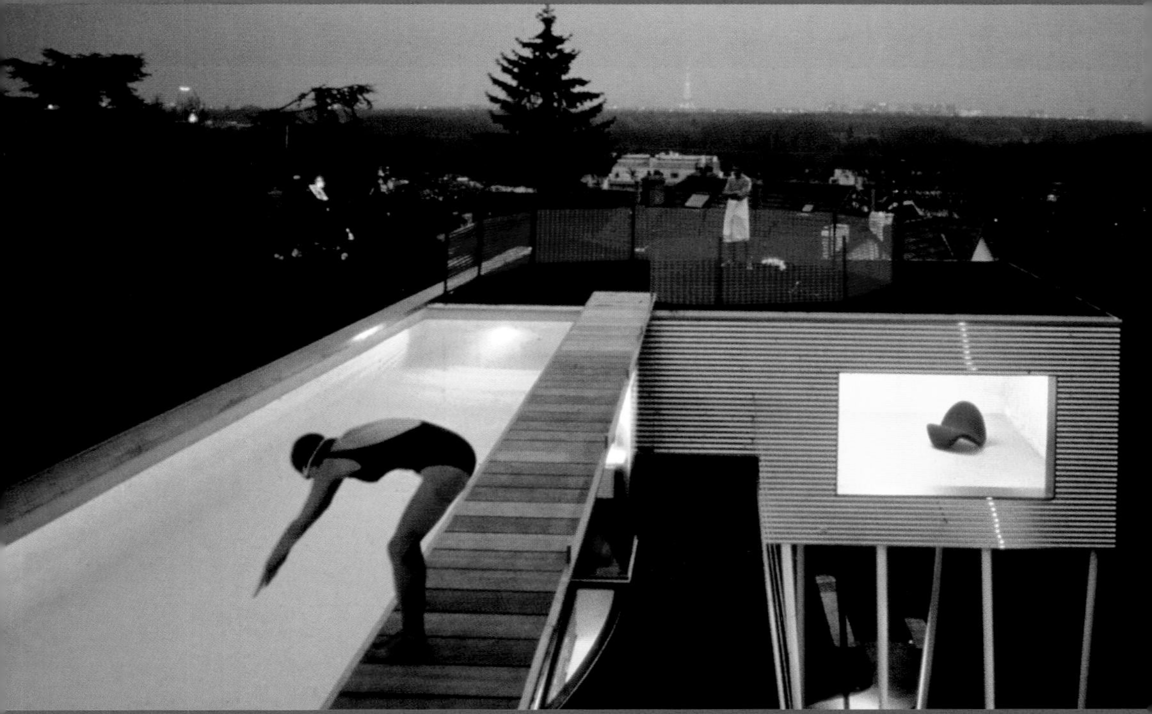

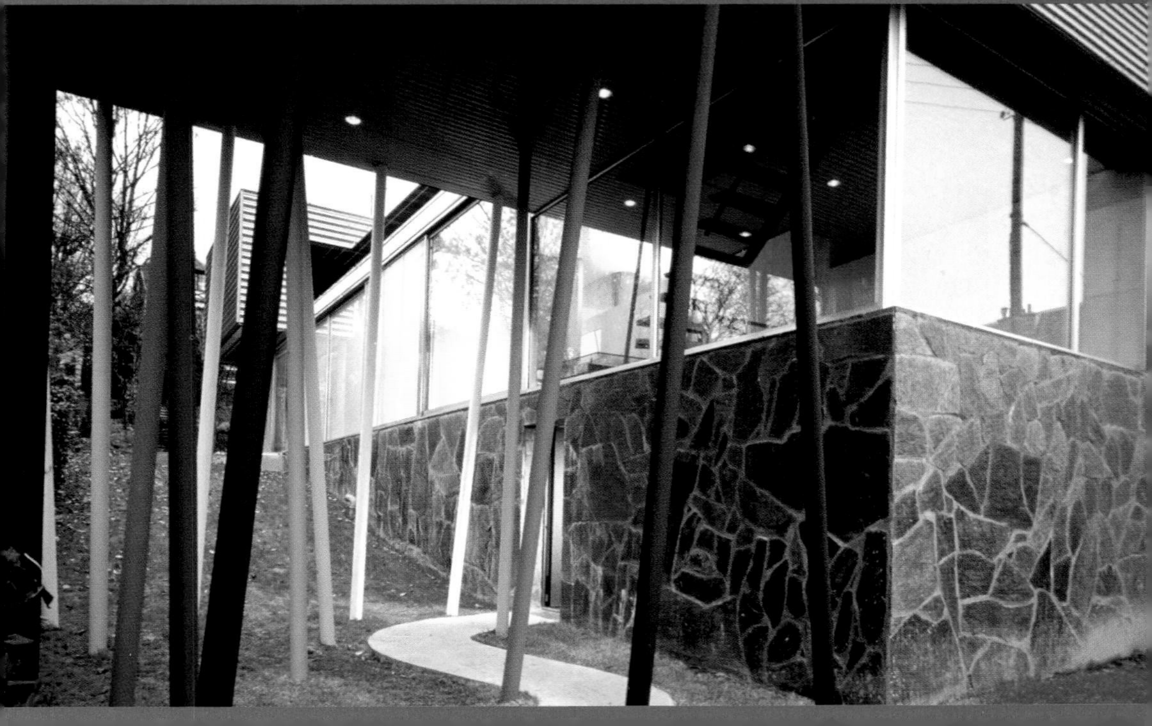

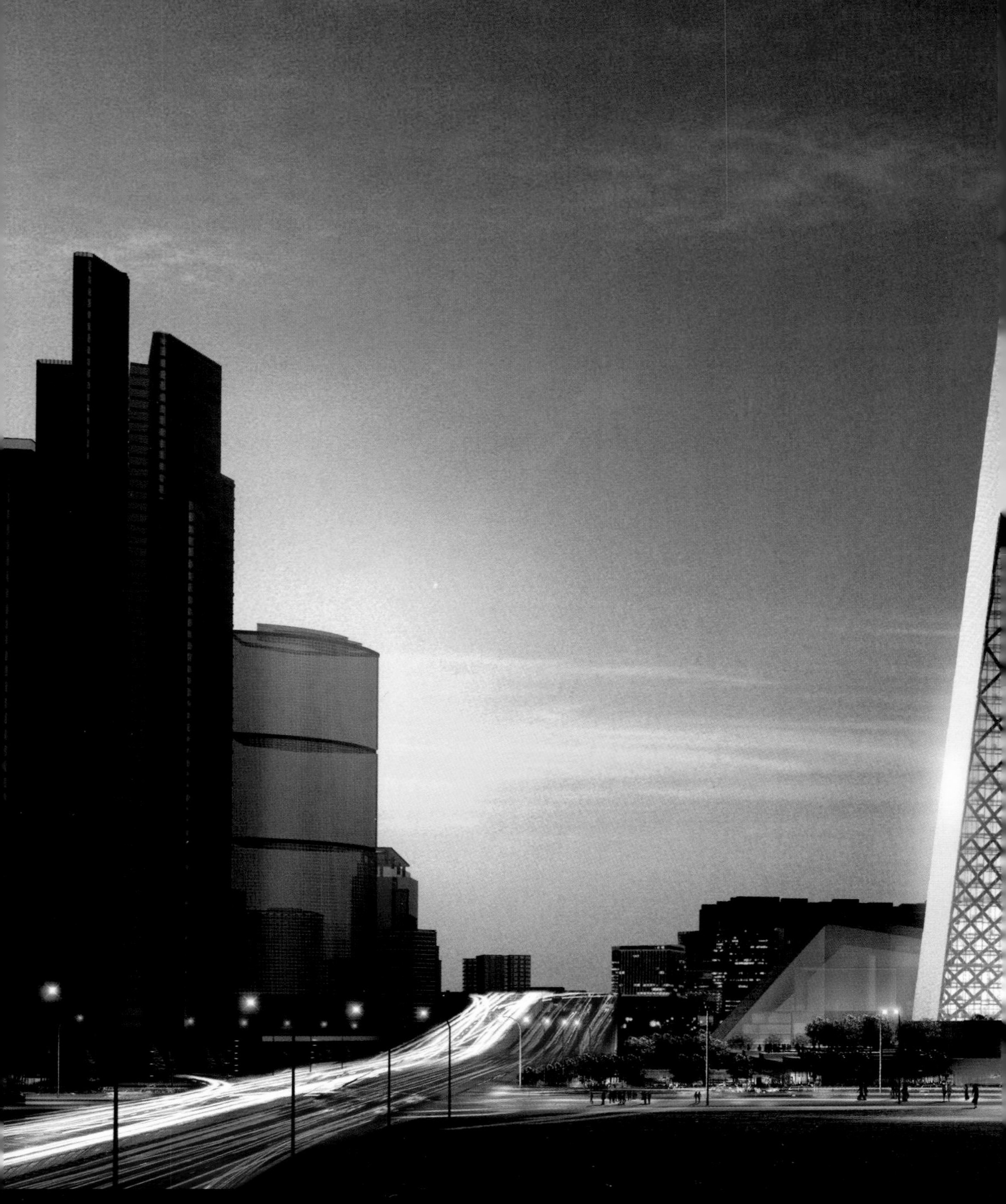

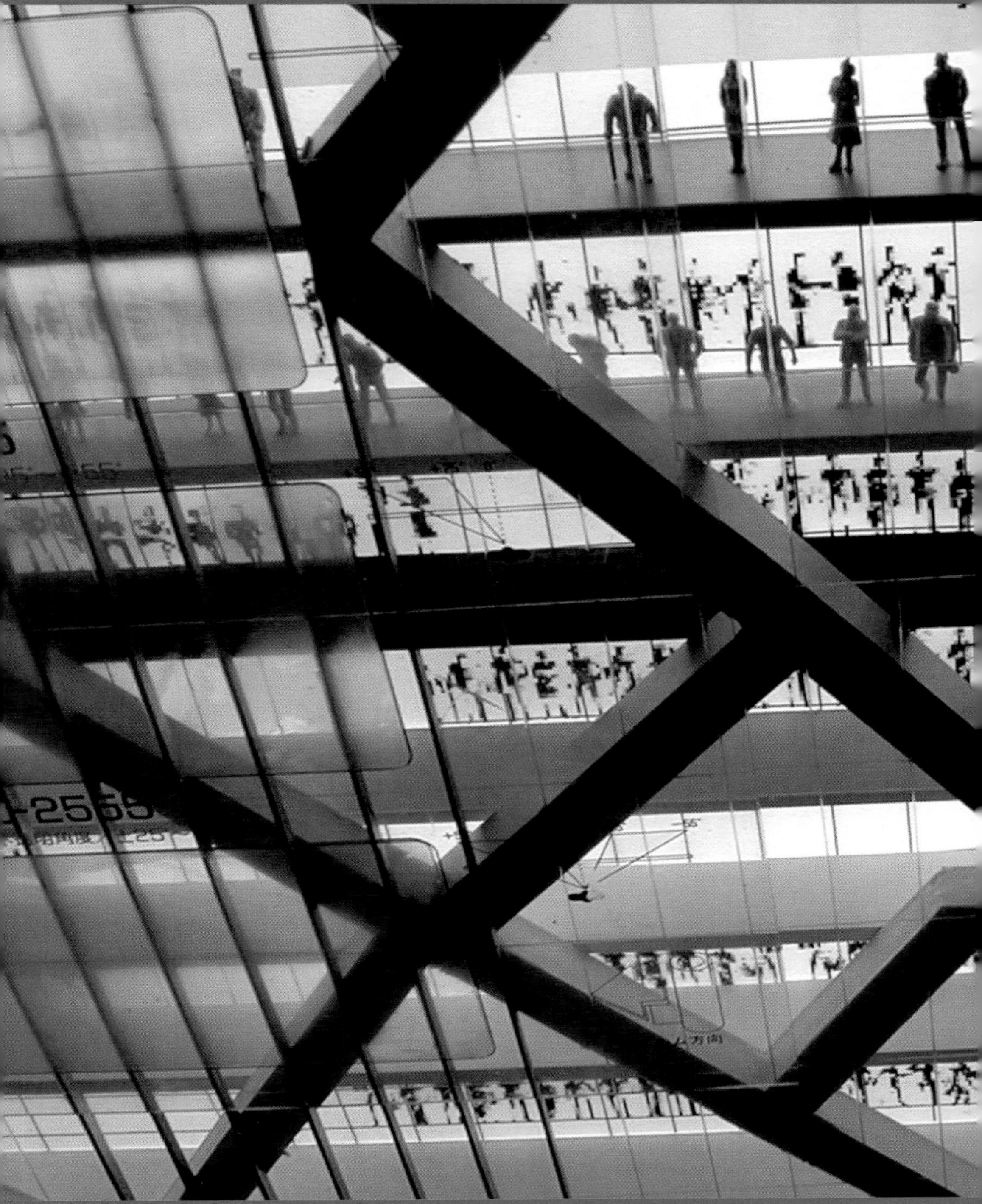

●RBIT

Aaron Betsky
Michael Sorkin
H.J.A. Hofland
Jean Attali
Ian Buruma

Rem Koolhaas: The Fire of Manhattanism Inside the Iceberg of Modernism

Aaron Betsky

Against the 'regime of the ¥€$' and conditional space, against the bland-ishments of good form and the economies of large-scale development, Rem Koolhaas brandishes an arsenal of images. Not content to allow himself to be co-opted by capitalism, nor interested in the position of the marginal avant gardist, he has dived into the stream of mass pro-duced media and found, within the historic discipline of architecture itself, a way of constructing an alternative, if tenuous post from which one can establish a critical position in late modernism: the pose of the architect as mythic maker, manipulator and mirror of data-driven imagery.

These days, it matters as much how an architect positions himself as it does what he makes. That is not because it is difficult to build or because architecture has failed to escape from the clutches of the fash-ion cycle, but because the accomplishment of any task in our society, whether it is writing a piece of criticism or selling a product or organis-ing a large corporate entity, is dependent not so much on production as it is on the mixture of branding, signature, sound-bite and image that creates the memorable moments of comprehension in an increasingly abstract economic and social system.[1]

Ironically, the image of the architect in our culture veers between the hip and the helacious. At times, the architect is the most smartly dressed avatar of urban chic, dashing from meeting to drawing table to building site to somehow arrange for the appearance of structures. As he is portrayed in Hollywood movies and television series, what he produces is usually not important, unless disaster strikes. The skyscraper or home on which he (never she) works is usually never shown. It is the image of the arranger that stands in the foreground.[2]

For those who have to live with the results of what the architect in actuality does, the image is the reverse. For neighbourhood action groups, the architect is usually the servile, but also imperious handmaiden of capitalism willingly placing large structures where they don't belong, producing wind and shadow and appropriating views, while causing more noise, traffic and other phenomena that are felt to diminish quality of life. Nor is the image of the architect much better to clients: he is usually seen as a diva-like artist pursuing his own goals at the expense of those who have to live in and with the results. Always exceeding budgets and time limits, he make structures that are often difficult to use and uncomfortable.

1. In this environment, the architect is just one of a group of 'identity providers' who help establish a sense of place or community, however fleetingly, for a targeted group of consumers. 'Star architects' then rise above these targeted and local concerns to be able to compete with media stars as shapers of global 'brands' or images. Unfortunately, a well-grounded description of the place of architecture in this economy is still to be written. For a description of the global economy and the place of information services, see Saskia Sassen, *The Global City: New York, London, Tokyo,* New York 2001. For branding, see Herbert Meyers and Richard Gerstman (eds.), *Branding @ the Digital Age,* New York 2002. For the role of 'symbolic analysts' within this economy, see Robert Reich, *The Work of Nations: Preparing Ourselves for 21st Century Capitalism,* New York 1992.
2. Cf. Andrew Saint, *The Image of the Architect,* New Haven 1985; Dana Cuff, *Architecture: The Story of a Practice,* Cambridge, Mass 1992; Judith R. Blau, *Architects and Firms: A Sociological Perspective on Architectural Practice,* Cambridge, Mass 1984.

Within the architecture world itself, the architect is seen as a victim, pursuing dreams of a perfect world while fending off the desires of clients to do things cheaply and meanly, trying to communicate the importance of good design to an uncomprehending public, working countless hours in search of ever greater perfection, and refusing to build any easy solutions. Underpaid and overworked, neither appreciated as an artist nor respected as a businessman, the architect sees himself as languishing forever somewhere in-between the real world in which he must build and the castles in the air he would like to construct.

To this particular triad of perceptions and self-perceptions, in which the architect has been caught since at least the middle of the nineteenth century (if not long before that), Rem Koolhaas and several of his contemporaries have added an alternative: the architect as the conscious collector, manipulator and projector of images. Though he cannot quite escape from criticism by users, clients and neighbours, he has fashioned a practice that does not allow it to be judged by those criteria. Though he plays the role of the dashing half-businessman, half-artist jetting around the globe, he has turned that image into a self-conscious construct. Though he – like almost all architects – complains about not being understood or receiving the right commissions, he leads a firm that does not limit its self-defined mission to the construction of buildings. He has created, for better or worse, something that is both a brand and a critical signature at the same time.[3]

Koolhaas's work consists of a number of agendas. The first is the writing (or drawing) of the myth of the late twentieth-century city.[4] The second is the composing, mainly in graphic terms, of the image of the post-urban, post-local twenty-first century urban agglomeration or

3. For the most acute description of how Koolhaas sees himself and is seen by his surroundings, see Arthur Lubow, 'How Architecture Rediscovered the Futur', *The New York Times Sunday Magazine,* 18 May 2003.

metropolis. The third is projection of the image of the architect as the self-conscious fulcrum of both that historic type and its proposed future alternative. To accomplish the last task, Koolhaas uses or attracts (though often at the same time denying) new models for the architect: the surfer, the pragmatic philosopher, the couturier for minimalist urban nomads. In the end, the success or failure of the buildings he has designed, though many of them are magnificent, may make less of a contribution to the future of architecture than the skilful and perhaps unconscious balancing act in which he engages in the construction of the new image of the architect.

The historical ground Koolhaas has constructed has two seemingly contradictory impulses. The first is a narrative about the hero architect able to condense, shape and celebrate urbanism in highly allusive form. The second is the obsessive gathering of statistical data in order to ground architecture not in form, but in analysis and prognosis. Early in his career, Koolhaas even found an image that encompasses these two tendencies: 'the fire of Manhattanism burning in the iceberg of modernism'.[5] Manhattan here stands for the myth of urbanity, a fetid stew of human culture, an artificial world somewhere between heaven and hell that is the exalted version of our body. Modernism is our mind, the cool realm of data, rationality and organisation that tends towards what Ludwig Mies van der Rohe called 'almost nothing'.

4. By myth I here mean a narrative description that uses a well-established, fairy-tale like structure, turning around iconic characters, moments and places, that evokes a world existing outside of time and place, and in which morality and other systems of judgment applicable in the here and now are not always relevant, but that acts as a validating or transforming story for a culture. See Eleazar M. Meletinsky, *The Poetics of Myth*, translated by Alexander Sadetsky and Guy Lanoue, New York 2000; Northrop Frye, *Myth and Metaphor*, Charlottesville, VA 1992.

5. Rem Koolhaas, *Delirious New York: A Retroactive Manifesto for Manhattan*, Oxford 1978, p. 171. For another viewpoint of New York Architecture in the same period, see Robert A.M. Stern, Gregory Gilmartin and Thomas Mellons, *New York 1930: Architecture and Urbanism between the Two World Wars*, New York 1987. Also of note are the many novels in which New York becomes a mythic city not unlike Koolhaas's vision. Examples include Mark Halprin, *A Winter's Tale*, New York 1984 and Steven Millhauser, *Martin Dressler*, New York 1999.

The *locus classicus* within the Koolhaas *œuvre* for the heroic myth of architecture is his first book, *Delirious New York*. Here, Koolhaas argues that it was a succession of architects, trained in classical forms but also in the ways of business, fluent in the social mores of their time, and possessing a vision of a new kind of city, who gave form to what we now think of as the essential New York. To Koolhaas, this is not just the competitive battle of skyscraper spires, but also the condensation of the whole known, human-made universe into the multipurpose confines of the gridded block out of which those stairways to heaven rise. Perfected in such towers as the Chrysler and Empire State Buildings, it turned into an urban strategy in Rockefeller Center before exploding in the post-Second World War era in projects such as that for the United Nations headquarters. Implicit in *Delirious New York* is that the resulting forms are now scattered around the world, ready to be picked up, reassembled and carried forward by the true heirs to the heroic generation of the pre-Depression era. In the theoretical projects at the end of the book, and in subsequent schemes for London and Rotterdam, Koolhaas staked his claim as one of those heirs.[6]

This image had the advantage of combining the modernist belief in architecture as social, economic and formal condenser dissolving into economic planning with the cloak of signifying form Postmodernists wished to throw over such skeletons. Moreover, the Koolhaasian architect was a self-conscious master builder, modelling himself on heroic figures whose world was neither all rational, nor all fictional, but properly mythic: larger than life, without moral compunction, but with an unarticulable end, and convincing by the very sublimity of the imagery they produced.

6. *Delirious New York*, op.cit. For a description of his architecture in the period immediately after the founding of the Office of Metropolitan Architecture, see David Block (ed.), *OMA: Rem Koolhaas Architecture 1970-1990*, New York 1996.

This myth of the metropolis, tied to its artifactor, rather than to some archaic sense of place or an image of the ruler, is not altogether new. In the case of New York, it had been erected by Robert Caro around Robert Moses,[7] and it certainly clings to Hausmann's Paris and Schinkel's Berlin.[8] What is new is that Koolhaas has extracted an essence of metro-politanism that is portable and packagable. It is the image of the com-pact, conflicted, glamorous, decadent city, thrusting up to the sky in tow-ers, laid out in a grid, defined by hidden services and made coherent by a shared culture, that can, in the end, be built anywhere in the world. It is this mythic, non-utopian, and perhaps notional city that still remains Koolhaas's greatest invention: 'The metropolis strives to reach a mythi-cal point where the world is completely fabricated by man, so that it absolutely coincides with his desires. The Metropolis is an addictive machine, from which there is no escape, unless it offers that, too …'[9]

While Koolhaas succeeded in constructing some of this continuations of Manhattanism, most notably in the Euralille project of 1988 to 1994, he also managed to create a epic bible to that mythos in his 1995 tome *S,M,L,XL*.[10] The tales of a mythic architecture are partially told, as are the images of the heroic figure, at times appearing naked like a classical god. The sheer size of the volume, its anti-narrative stance, and its seduc-tive appearance (stage managed by graphic designer Bruce Mau) made it the prime reference point for a generation of architects growing up in an era in which Cold War conflict and economic recession had given way to the emergence of new political, social and economic structures that

7. Robert A. Caro, *The Power Broker: Robert Moses and the Fall of New York*, New York 1975.
8. Cf. John Zukowsky, Birgit Verwiebe and Kurt Forster (eds.), *Karl Friedrich Schinkel 1781-1841: The Drama of Architecture*, New York 1995; David P. Jordan, *Transforming Paris: The Life and Labors of Baron Haussman*, Chicago 1996.
9. *Delirious New York*, p. 293.
10. Rem Koolhaas, *S,M,L,XL*, New York/Rotterdam 1995. The book starts with the observation that 'Architecture is a hazardous mix of omnipotence and impotence' (p. xix).

seemed to call for the fragmented, but heroic modernism Koolhaas had espoused.

It is important in this regard that Koolhaas himself consciously eschewed style. He did this by relying for the actual visual appearance and tactile immediacy of his buildings on a wide array of collaborators (Petra Blaise, Joep van Lieshout, and Maarten van Seeveren, to name just a few), while continually and consistently repudiating the work of any of his former employees or students that resembled any of his own projects.[11] His buildings tended towards insubstantiality as well as a denial of proper structural distinctions, not in the manner of modernist reduction, but by continually frustrating what is proper ('no money, no detail', he is famous for saying) and what is expected (floors sliding into walls, rooms sliding between floors). He tried – again, whether consciously or not is unclear – to make things that would be considered ugly by most accepted canons of good taste: rubber and plastic materials used for luxurious coverings, buildings that were top-heavy, shapes that were out of kilter. Similarly, his statements were slippery, never aligning himself with any movement, but maintaining a critical distance. Exactly by not allowing his buildings to locate themselves anywhere in a consensus of good taste or acceptability, while providing enough internal coherence and external references to make sense, he was able to allow them to exist as tantalising images seemingly forever balancing at the edge of realisation.[12]

This complex and continual juggling act, necessary to release the architect from the bounds of expectations in which he might otherwise

---

11. Cf. Bernard Colenbrander and Jos Bosman (eds.), *Reference: OMA: The Sublime Start of an Architectural Generation,* translated by Victor Joseph, Rotterdam 1995.

12. Koolhaas is certainly not alone in pursuing strategies that question the supremacy of good taste, proposing that criticality might begin with the rejection of such middle class, enlightenment-generated values. For a recent celebration of such 'unformed' counterproposals, see Yve-Alain Bois, *L'Informe: Mode d'Emploi,* Paris 1998. See also Lesley Hall Higgins, *The Modernist Cult of Ugliness: Aesthetic and Gender Politics,* New York 2002.

be caught, only works because of Koolhaas's continual reliance on data. Early in his career, he studied such institutions as the Regional Plan Association in New York, but he also assimilated a Dutch tradition in which the architect is a collector and manipulator of social and economic data. Initiated by a group of architects who wished to take the Bauhaus ideals of working with and through industrialisation to its logical next step, and allied to such efforts at graphic rationalisation as Otto Neurath's Universal Sign Language, it was a planning process that was made famous by the architect Cor van Eesteren after the Second World War. In Van Eesteren's plans for the expansion of Amsterdam and the planning of the new IJsselmeer polders, physical form was supposed to be the result of a reliance on data collected by the various institutions of the Dutch state. This collecting itself had a long history, going back to at least the sixteenth century, but in the post-war era reached its apogee in the belief in the 'makeable civilisation'. Analysis and projection would allow planners to harness industry and capital not just within the contours of a four- or five-year plan, but in order to steer, guide and shape the 'spatial organisation' of the country.[13]

The Dutch were of course by no means alone in these efforts. The German mania for collecting data culminated in the Second World War, when Hitler's favourite architect, Albert Speer, could effortlessly make the transition from producing heroic forms for a future Berlin to coordinating concentration camp transports, because underlying both was the ability to organise data in order to produce 'almost nothing': immensely huge and abstract buildings or mass annihilation. In a less horrid sense, the American architects of the post-war era, such as

13. Cf. Vincent van Rossem, *Het Algemeen Uitbreidingsplan van Amsterdam: Geschiedenis en Ontwerp*, Rotterdam 1993, pp. 100ff. The relationship between this work and a recent generation of architects has been explored by Bart Lootsma, most recently in 'What is (Really) To Be Done', in Véronique Patteeuw (ed.), *Reading MVRDV*, Rotterdam 2003, pp. 24-63, pp. 37-41.

Skidmore, Owings and Merrill, were above all coordinators of information who presented their finished products as the very image or rational planning. The grid, which in Koolhaas's image of pre-war New York was still the generator of polymorphously perverse forms, was now merely a sign of a corporatist state.

Though Koolhaas cites as his models those architects, such as Wallace K. Harrison,[14] or Hugh Maaskant,[15] who proposed heroic form instead of modular planning, his early work was heavily shaped by the planning processes in which buildings such as his Amsterdam North housing took shape. During the 1980s, probably as a result of the challenges of the Euralille project, Koolhaas began generating his own research. Over time, his efforts intensified, including not just the usual kinds of population and econometric data proper to planning, but even the hours he himself spent in airplanes. This data was given shape through graphic design. Though that had been the case in the pre-Second World War era, the declarative form of data imaging had been lost in the Netherlands, but was brought to Koolhaas's office through graphic designers such as Mau and later Michael Rock, who were consciously looking at that tradition.[16]

Graphic design and the organisation of data into image that was not translated into something else, but was only the collection, organisation, emphasis and abstract translation of data itself, provided Koolhaas with an antidote to the notion that architecture must somehow, despite itself, lead to form. Data as form, whether it was the American grid or the Dutch 'stamp' out of which housing projects were generated, had become

14. Cf. Victoria Newhouse, *Wallace K. Harrison*, Architect, New York 1989.
15. Cf. Michelle Provoost, *Maaskant*, Rotterdam 2003.
16. There is as of yet no good critical analysis of Dutch graphic design of the last few decades. For a general introduction, see Kees Broos and Paul Hefting, *Een Eeuw Grafische Vormgeving in Nederland*, Amsterdam 1993. For a survey of recent work, see Ramon Prat and Tomoko Sakamoto (eds.), *HD: Holland Design New Graphics*, Barcelona 2001.

a sign – and a generally negative one – for bureaucracy. Through skilful and declarative graphic design, data could become heroic again. It could have the quality of El Lissitzky's *Beat the White Square with the Red Wedge:* its very form could be political.[17]

The rediscovery of agitprop as a tool of visual criticism in the U.S. by designers such as Tibor Kalman and in the Netherlands by groups such as Hard Werken en Wild Plakken later received a structure through the theories of Edward Tufte and Richard Saul Wurman,[18] who emphasised the best ways in which graphic designers could convey information. A new visual language was born that was an equivalent and reversal of 'the fire of Manhattanism burning inside the iceberg of modernism': the clinical precision of data collection and analysis was represented with the hot type and bold forms of charts and sans-serif lines of information.

Koolhaas adopted and adapted this methodology, creating an architecture that was itself a form of three-dimensional graphic design. It was an architecture that dissolved into data, or rather surfed on it. Here Koolhaas had found an answer to the question of what happens to form after it has been reduced to a Miesian 'almost nothing', both by the internal logic of architecture history (in which it shares the logic of ever greater abstraction with painting and sculpture) and the corrosive effects of economic rationalisation, which continually reduce the need for expensive, expressive form. Architecture could become a key element in the Information Era that began clearly dawning at the beginning of the

17. The relationship between graphic design and propaganda is explored in an ongoing manner in the *Journal of Popular Culture,* published by the Wolfsonian in Miami Beach. See also Robert Philippe, *Political Graphics: Art as a Weapon,* New York 1982. For Bruce Mau's use of this tradition, see Bruce Mau, *Life Style,* London 2000.
18. Edward R. Tufte, *Envisioning Information,* New Haven 1990 and *The Visual Display of Quantitative Information,* New Haven 2001, Richard Saul Wurman, *Information Anxiety,* New York 1989 and *Envisioning USA,* Newport, RI 1999.
19. See *Wired Magazine* issue, June 2003.

1990s. The architect would be able not just to collect information, but to give it shape in a way that was proper to its own logic. Buildings would no longer be the tombs of information that had led to their construction, but open structures allowing for the continual manipulation and ordering of data. These open structures, continuous and almost invisible, would offer recognition and visual order by bathing themselves in the natural products of data manipulation, the free-floating projections thrown up by electronic media. Such was certainly the dream of such pivotal projects as the Jussieu Library in Paris and the ZKM in Karlsruhe. This does not mean that the buildings were a-spatial. In fact, the complexity of the structures Koolhaas and OMA started producing after around 1992 (when the Kunsthal in Rotterdam was completed) takes the essential step of making abstractions palpable. It is as if the dreams of the 'cyberpunk' fiction of the same era, in which we would all cruise through immense and rich realms of data, here found their building blocks.

It also meant that the architect was no longer just a designer of buildings. Koolhaas had sold a controlling interest in his firm in 1996 to a large engineering company, and thus the making of buildings was something he did, in a manner, as a hired consultant. Shortly after this, he started AMO, the reverse of his firm (Office for Metropolitan Architecture, or OMA), and intensified his independent research projects. Initially tied to his professorship at Harvard University, they soon ranged to consultancies for Conde Nast Magazines[19] and the European Economic Community[20] in which exactly the way in which information found its way into form was central.

The field of operation also extended from more-or-less traditional analysis of cities such as Hong Kong to larger areas (the whole Pearl River Delta)[21] and phenomena (shopping)[22] that clearly exceeded the ability of the traditional architect to 'do something' with or about them.

Koolhaas did not go in to see poverty or lack of infrastructure and then propose a system that would solve these deficiencies. He mainly photographed and collected seemingly random statistics and piquant details meant to shock and amaze (the amount of highways being built in the Pearl River Delta,[23] their ownership by a Hong Kong businessman who funded a building designed by Robert Venturi at Princeton University;[24] the self-organising market in Lagos, photographed as the realisation of such ideas about non-linear forms of coherence[25]).

The lectures, books, articles and even products – such as a proposed new brand for the European Economic Community that is a condensation of the constituent countries' national flags but looks like a bar code – produced under the aegis of AMO elevate graphic design to the status of architectural surfing or the surfing form of criticism into clear, concise imagery. The architect was now someone who used his knowledge of the history and constituent elements of such phenomena to analyse them and reflect this new knowledge or data in forms that were proper to the medium itself, that is, graphic, unstable and virtual. Veering between the 'information architecture' of Richard Saul Wurman and the neo-realist imaging of the post-Becher school of photographers,[26] Koolhaas began producing an architecture of information.

Yet Koolhaas never let go of the notion that such data must be fit into a myth. At times, he seemed to be groping towards the positioning of such a myth by analysing ever more exotic and dangerous locales (such as Lagos, Nigeria) and by producing seductive, but open-ended criticisms

20. European Union and Brussels as Capital, AMO study, 2002.
21. Cf., Rem Koolhaas et.al. (eds.), *The Great Leap Forward*, Cologne 2002.
22. Cf. Rem Koolhaas et.al. (eds.), *The Harvard Guide to Shopping*, Cologne 2002.
23. Ibid. 21.
24. The developer of toll roads is Gordon Wu, who donated a hall with his name on it to Princeton University.
25. Lagos documentary, 2002.
26. Prominent members of this school include Andreas Gursky and Thomas Struth.
27. Rem Koolhaas (ed.), *Projects for Prada Part 1*, Milan 2001.

('all conditioned space is conditional', 'the regime of the ¥€$') that implied, but never stated, an alternative position. By now one of the most famous and successful architects in the world, he was balancing on the edge of how mythic the modern architect could be without committing himself to one or another kind of building practice.

The answer to his dilemma came in the form of the fashion house Prada. For the former Maoist Muccia Prada and her late-capitalist venture conglomerator husband, Koolhaas produced not so much buildings or analyses, as conduits for fashion. At first, he treated the project as a continuation of his research work, collecting data about shopping patterns. He then combined this data and its graphic translation with his passion for experimental materials and forms. The result was a proposed real estate strategy, a visual vocabulary, and a range of modular display systems. He also brought in equally strong and famous architects, such as Herzog & de Meuron, to collaborate on the actual buildings in what was to be the making of an open-ended system that would allow Prada to spread throughout the world. The anchor for this particular set of castles in the air was Prada's own self-conscious, backward-looking minimalism that grounded efficient, rational design in craft and recognisable images. Lifestyle, Prada-style, was pure minimalism as an assertive, graphic appearance. It was the uniform for the symbolic analyst cruising the globe, the prefect sign for the human being as intersection of information at a point of desire. Just as important, however, was the complete divorce between the cost of the products and the surplus value Prada was able to liberate from them, which was out of proportion even within the world of high fashion.[27]

The seemingly unending funds, the continually self-conscious minimalism and high craft, and the willingness to comment on and construct this world as a series of buildings let Koolhaas pose his work as the ultimate fashioning of modern life. He was not only dressing himself and those who would be like him, he was not only giving shape to a post-urban, global nomadic tribe and economic system, but he was also commenting on that whole effort within the image itself. Soon he was even designing advertising for Prada that included images of fakes being sold in Moscow's Red Square and photographs of the crowds at a Prada runway show with the actual models removed.[28] 'Lifestyle', the word that, together with 'branding' seemed to be the way to describe the lack of permanence, continuity or inherent value in almost any place, product or image that the information age seemed to engender through its continual shunting of data back and forth across the globe,[29] here became architecture. The fire of Manhattanism now burned inside the iceberg of the modernist runway model, or perhaps inside Koolhaas, standing in for the everyman urban nomad, himself. Lifestyle branding did not create a myth, but itself became a mythic activity.

And what now? Prada has, at least for the moment, imploded, as has the data bubble. 'We seem to be obsessed with making funny shapes these days', says one of his employees. Is Koolhaas then finally becoming a traditional architect who is 'just' designing recognisable shapes for libraries (Seattle), concert halls (Oporto) and broadcasting companies (CCTV) that, though each distinct and logical in their generation, share formal relations?[30]

It is not so easy to dismiss Rem Koolhaas. He has managed, as the only major architect working today, to propose the building blocks for a post-urban condition in which the essential elements of what makes a cohesive culture are dispersed more and more around the globe and

28. Prada Sport Advertisement Campaign, AMO, 2002.
29. The pervasive influence of 'lifestyle branding' has been most famously described by Naomi Klein in her *No Logo*, New York 2000; see also Thomas Klein, *The Conquest of Cool: Business Culture, Counterculture, and the Rise of Hip Consumerism*, Chicago 1997.
30. For a recent survey of these projects, see Rem Koolhaas (ed.), *Content*, Cologne 2003.

appear only as floating, unstable images. Architecture here is no longer just a question of building, but of condensing data into form that is both insubstantial (modernist) and seductive (Manhattanist) enough to become mythic. That is an ability Koolhaas has had for several decades, and that he continues to refine and develop. He liberated architecture from place, from its maker and even from materiality, without letting it disappear into nothing. He, along with certain modern artists, constructs images because it is images that can make sense of a power that is increasingly invisible, running through electrical wires or sitting in virtual accounts in banks. It recognises that, in an era in which value no longer inheres in physical properties or places, it is the adding and removing and value through intelligent systems, but also the ability to make such value real through image and form, that are successful positions in architecture. Combined, they have both the fleeting nature of fashion and also the convincing power of myth that will allow us to survive in the storms of images, data and grinding, physical and economic violence that swirl around us. Rem Koolhaas has used the image of architecture to produce a convincing architecture of image.

Recently, sitting in yet another panel about architecture and globalization, I listened to the Dutchman to my right metaphorize world culture as a huge ocean wave and offer – as an architectural strategy for dealing with it – the figure of the surfer, riding the crest. Although this image has certain détourning charm, the 'wave' model is all wet, camouflaging the reality of a constructed culture as a force of nature. Confronted by the massive sameness of sprawl – the urbanism of global capital – my colleague chose not to resist but to go with the flow, to invent it as the inevitable substrate of the whole world.

Ironically, this reappropriation of the fantasy of nature as a vast autonomous web of which we are not precisely a part comes at a moment when we are busily discovering our own enormous impact on the natural environment, its fragility in the face of our won activities. Global warming, the rapid disappearance of habitats and ecosystems, worldwide pollution, and the breakneck homogenization of the built environment are all symptomatic of a world in which we can no more consider ourselves simply another species than we can stand raptly outside it, shivering at its majesty.

The view of my fellow panelist was deeply romantic, aspiring to a kind of post-technological sublimity. For him, the onrush of globalization was merely irresistible, it had an aesthetic authority in its deep imprinting of power on form. Such 'generic' urbanism – the architecture of the wave – represented an unavoidable default, a condition growing autonomously, throwing up its endlessness of freeways and airports, office towers and gated communities, McDonald's and KFCs. The surfer epistemology panders to this updated universality with a canny resignation of agency and, hence, responsibility.

Identity as Handicap

H.J.A. Hofland

Rem Koolhaas is one of my best discoveries. This happy accident happened to me in 1978. I was in New York, living in Brooklyn in a big, old hotel at the end of Montague Street, close to Brooklyn Heights. It is now owned by Jehovah's Witnesses, but at the time it was in the last days of its fading gentility – a reception desk manned by old gentlemen in threadbare suits, a decrepit lift cage encased by the stairwells, and rooms with all mod cons but whose porcelain fixtures were a mosaic of brown cracks. At the other end of Montague Street is the Borough Hall subway station. The number 3 train, an express, gets you to the Chambers Street station in a few minutes, where you can transfer onto the local, to Canal, or Sheridan Square, or into Midtown in about 10 minutes. I can never praise the raw efficiency of this metropolitan public transport system highly enough.

On these trains, one reads. I read The *New York Review of Books,* and in it a long discussion of *Delirious New York, A Retroactive Manifesto for Manhattan.* The reviewer displayed a sometimes sceptical undertone, but for the most part, approbation and a sense of surprised admiration predominated. This detailed story aroused my curiosity, and because it was about a compatriot, a sense of pride as well, for within the limits of the detachment of moderates I am a patriot and nationalist. What Dutchman would get several pages in the *Review* about his book? I bought a copy at the Dalton Bookstore, walked over to Washington Square Park and started reading. It was a melancholy morning in early autumn, the most gorgeous Indian Summer, the kind you only get in New York. It is always best to read about cities, people, battles in their actual settings. It fuels the imagination. About the First World War in northern France, about Napoleon in Moscow, and about Manhattan in Manhattan.

The programme of this book is spelled out from the eighth line of the introduction. 'Manhattan is the 20th century's Rosetta Stone.' The programme for decoding. And one page later: 'Manhattan's architecture is a paradigm for the exploitation of congestion.' A number of artists have given their diagnosis on Manhattan in their own ways. My clear favourite is Saul Steinberg, who studied architecture before he discovered his own genius. He painted Manhattan, among other things, as a collection of ant-hills, inhabitants streaming out of the buildings. The Emperor Hotel, the photograph of a Biedermeier diner, on a street otherwise lined with shoebox buildings, some encased in a torn burlap bag. Manhattan observed. As I read Koolhaas's vision of congestion, Steinberg's vision came to me. Today I reread the introduction and the first chapter. I stop reading after this sentence: 'Manhattan is an accumulation of possible disasters that never happen.' There is no perceptible line between intuition and prophecy.

Then, 25 years ago, I got to the chapter in *Delirious New York* on Coney Island. Three epigrams precede it, all good, but I will quote only the best, the last one, by Maxim Gorky: 'Hell is very badly done.' I kept reading, entranced. What was I doing sitting on that bench, near that undersized Arc de Triomphe, between two homeless people. I had never seen Coney Island. I caught the subway, travelling through the urban wastelands of East New York, the wooden houses, the rows of electricity poles, the brick factories, water towers, a pool of mud, depots of old rust, the fantastic *terrain vague* or wasteland of what is now called 'modernity'.

End of the line. A megacavern of a station. And there again the faintly hazy light of an autumn day. Surf Avenue, with, a stone's throw away on the right, the surrealistic structure of rails and beams of the big roller coaster, the Thunderbolt. It was about a five-minute walk along the deserted, dejected machine park of amusement, guarded by pit bulls, to the Boardwalk, the elevated wooden boulevard that lines the beach on the land side. I read through the first chapter of *Delirious New York* there on a bench – the account, the reconstruction of the minutely designed, logically carried out dream of the insane. This happened while the avant-gardists plotted and carried out their rebellion in Russia, Marinetti developed his cult of the race car, Duchamp fastened his bicycle wheel on a stool, the progression toward Dada and surrealism was in its first phase of acceleration. During the same period, on Coney Island, popular surrealism reached a stage of development that perhaps has never been surpassed.

I read. I looked around me. There was where Luna Park had stretched, Dreamland; there was where the Leap Frog Railway had ridden. Never before had mortals so vigorously competed with the Creator, their only aim to liberate their customers, for a fee, from that other Creation, completely, by suspending the laws of nature. There, to paraphrase another Gorky epigram used by Koolhaas, man had been stripped of his own shadow. Only on Coney Island did the word surrealism come so close to its literal meaning. Coney Island, dating from before the First World War, as evoked in *Delirious New York,* is the first attempt to use technology to

achieve a total grasp on everything, including the playfulness, the imagination of millions. It is impossible to conceive a greater supremacy. This
is encapsulated in the picture that Koolhaas evokes of this surrealistic
mini-state.

There are some artists – painters, writers, architects – who, united by
a particular drive, and unrelated to their talent or genius, are a breed
apart. They are driven toward the all-encompassing. Jonathan Swift created his own planet in *Gulliver's Travels,* refashioned human beings,
grouped them into races, gave them their own mores and customs, made
them inhabit specially designed states, all in order to give existing human
beings a clearer picture of their own existence. Leonardo Da Vinci was
restlessly occupied in a different way. He designed weapons, churches,
machines, medical instruments, painted and wrote, and did far more
things besides than can be named. He dabbled in everything; his collected notes are a monument to universal meddlesomeness. Yet another
example: Aldous Huxley in his *Brave New World,* more than an anti-
Utopia – the product of logical thinking about plausible progress in medical science and engineering in combination with a conceivable development of ideology.

Swift, Leonardo and Huxley are outstanding examples. They belong
to the breed of artists that are obsessed throughout their lives by the
ever-present desire somehow to encompass the universe, one way or
another, and record it in their work. This might be in a novel, a painting, a philosophical system, but also in a single sentence, a single object,
a single insight, a single invention. They have to try, time and time again.
The compulsion is there, independent of the talent. Their work as a
whole is a manifesto.

(This is not to detract from artists who belong to the other breed.
This breed is not any less ambitious, just fundamentally different, and
we find among them talents of no lesser distinction. They see through

their model, they make their ideas reality, and that is that. It is another way of creating a beautiful body of work. The difference is that the magic of the hunkering for the universal is missing.)

With the chapter on Coney Island, Koolhaas charted the course, indicated the direction of the historical enquiry, determined the choice of witnesses, set the tone. *Delirious New York* evolves before the reader's eyes into a manifesto, and reading it in its setting, or remembering what he read a short time before, the reader suddenly sees the manifest made evident at every turn. Manhattan itself is a manifestation of this universe I referred to above. And that was my conclusion at the time: the writer-architect achieved identification with the city in this book.

In 1995, *Small, Medium, Large, Extra Large* was published – 1,345 pages, one and a half kilos. The first sentence confirmed my diagnosis of Koolhaas and the universe: 'Architecture is a hazardous mixture of omnipotence and impotence.' And further on: 'In other words, this is a painfully utopian enterprise.' Speaking very personally, I think this is a magnificent book, a repository of discoveries, ideas, plans, snapshots and pictures, genres, insights and outlooks, aphorisms, a glossary – infectious in the energy contained within it, challenging in the impertinence with which it deals with all of humanity in its existence, its present, past and future. A three-dimensional labyrinth with no blind alleys. In this respect *S,M,L,XL* is a mad book, comparable in its thoroughness to the *Opperlanse Taal- en Letterkunde* tome by Battus on Dutch wordplay, which also includes everything, albeit in a different domain.

I will limit myself to what I consider a key essay, 'The Generic City', written in 1994. It starts on page 1238, and it too still reads, almost 10 years later, like a manifesto – in this case not retroactive but in progress. And as is proper for a manifesto, it begins with a powerful assault on established thinking. Identity! Our cherished hallmark of existence. An illusion. 'Identity is like a mousetrap in which more and more mice have to share the original bait. … The stronger the identity, the more it imprisons, the more it resists expansion, interpretation, renewal, contradiction.' And the essay-manifesto goes on to lay out the brilliant, startling elaboration of this thesis.

The generic city. Let us consult our experience, step outside ourselves, look at the way in which we exist, how our work, habitation, play or entertainment is continuously being reorganized, how the city changes before our very eyes, irrespective of our personal tastes, views, or political choice. Realize that we have been assigned the role of the mass in the new pageant-play of permanent revolution, which has no authors. Koolhaas: 'The Generic City presents the final death of planning. Why? Not because it is not planned – in fact, huge complementary universes of bureaucrats and developers funnel unimaginable flows of energy and money into its completion; for the same money, its plains can be fertilized by diamonds, its mud fields paved in gold bricks. … But its most dangerous and most exhilarating discovery is that planning makes no difference whatsoever.'

Yes, that is the absurdity of this revolution: we plan like mad, better and better instruments at our disposal; we restlessly start on the next painstakingly designed improvements. Doubt, ambition, competition, workshop, market forces, return on investment, conference, identity. All variable imponderables in the computer. Plan. Decision. Action. In the dictionary, on page 1024, there are three entries for 'plan'. The first: 'The Plan is the generator.' That I can immediately agree with. The plan is the foundation of any meaningful action. Building is one of the most meaningful actions human beings are capable of. Any plan worthy of the name comprises, within given limits, the visualisation of perfection. And from the very first moment, it is clear that the completed work will be different from the visualisation from which the work was generated.

Then the third entry: 'To invent a Plan. The Plan justifies you to such a degree that you can no longer be held accountable, not even for the Plan itself. Just throw the stone and hide your hand. If there really were a Plan, there would be no failure.' Nicely worded, but it rubs me the wrong way. The fact of the incongruity between the plan on the drawing board and what is implemented is the consequence of an initial failure of imagination and stubborn reality. View both, if need be, as flaws. That is simply the predictability of the unpredictable, also known as unforeseen circumstances. Yet the planner can never use this X factor, always known in advance, as justification for renouncing the authorship of his initiative. Should this be accepted (it is happening more and more all the time), then a different chaos results, in which anyone can serve as anyone else's scapegoat. That is the flipside of what is now becoming reality: the culture, the cycle of insurance policies, the claims, the 'I'll sue you. See you in court'. The damper on any sort of inventiveness and entrepreneurial drive.

This is different from the absurdity of revolution, which, as observed above by Koolhaas, leads to the discovery that all the planning in the world fails to produce any sort of order. We know that this is dangerous, and at the same time it can makes us laugh. Current reality, reduced to a play by Eugène Ionesco.

I am a Utopian. My flaw is that I confine myself to writing. In my daydreams, as I walk around the city, sit on public transport, ride the train across the country, I fantasise about big renovations, new designs, demolition and construction. I envy the architect and the urban planner, whose occupation it is to make people lead more functional lives. In the final analysis, it is unbelievable that architects and urban planners are granted the power to make countless masses move, day in and day out, along paths they have devised. How much better, then, to give them paths that are better than those that already exist.

Through a concurrence of historical surprises, we have arrived at an age devoid of ideology and devoid of Utopias. This period itself has no identity. I find myself amazed, almost every day, that in this void we are not experiencing a boom in Utopias. I am especially amazed at the lethargy, the fatalism with which the creative class is allowing this vacuum to wash over it. I read Le Corbusier, his …, yes, his manifesto *L'avion accuse,* written in 1935, in which he describes the function of the aeroplane. 'The aeroplane is an accusation, an indictment, a summons. It indicts the city. It indicts those who make decisions about the city. Thanks to the aeroplane we now have proof that architecture and urban planning must be changed.'

I encounter the same tone, the same urgency, the same untainted perception, leaping of ideas, drive to action, the undertone of haste in Rem Koolhaas. These times are crying out for Utopias. But who cries out? The flaw of this age is that we have forgotten how to cry out, unless it is to scream at and about what we already know. The scream as the most modern, the most universal of clichés. The scream as fulfilment, the precooked shriek of ecstasy as the ultimate profundity and wisdom. How is it possible that our teeming masses can consider this suffocating situation as a comfortable end point?

Koolhaas's thinking, combined with his building, is practical Utopia; laid down in his writing is the Utopia of incipient reality. This must perforce be done in a tone that apodictically precludes satisfaction, contentment, satiety. In these times, many people see Utopias as presumptuous. They are wrong. What is perceived as presumptuous here is in reality the disruption of the existing order, which would otherwise throttle itself.

When Koolhaas was awarded the Pritzker Architecture Prize (more or less considered the Nobel Prize for architecture), *The New York Times* called him the 'most influential architect of his generation'. The best newspaper in the world devoted an entire page to his work. In the

Netherlands they made do with a couple of column inches. Some fellow Dutch artists are sometimes described as 'world-famous in the Netherlands'; Koolhaas is an example of someone who is world-famous everywhere else in the world. Why is that?

The Netherlands is too modest. The Dutch language is replete with expressions that serve our ideology of humility. 'Pride cometh before a fall.' 'Cobbler, stick to thy last!' 'Don't step beyond your book!' 'Don't reach too high!' 'Know your limits!' 'Keep both feet on the ground!' 'Birds that sing too early are for the cat!' 'If you behave normally, you are quite mad enough.' 'Don't get any big ideas in your head.'

Free thinking in the Netherlands has voluntarily narrowed itself. It has bowed to two deadly foes: Saint Consensus and the Demon of Professional Jealousy (*jalousie de métier*). Rem Koolhaas keeps on working, as if they did not exist.

JEAN ATTALI, IN: LE PLAN ET LE DÉTAIL. UNE PHILOSOPHIE DE L'ARCHITECTURE ET DE LA VILLE,

NÎMES, 2001, PP. 101-102

Does one always begin from architecture in the attempt to understand the city, that is, to conceive urban space and evaluate its sociability? Or is the city as such what must offer and imagine a role for architecture? In the years that followed the abandonment of the CIAM's functionalist themes, when the architects of Team Ten exercised their influence, relayed soon after by Archigram in England and Archizoom Associati in Italy, it was possible to recognize both tendencies: and they persist even today.

The first is the spontaneous inclination of the architects themselves: the 'urban project' is the recurrent motif of a vision of territorial develop-ment, and of a claim to recover the former unity of the architect's role, against the fragmentation of technical capacities. A rather complacent ideal where the virtues of architectural drawing and dialogue with the inhabitants find the keys to a new harmony in the figure of the project leader: both a visionary and an intercessor. The second tendency, on the contrary, can only be taken up by architects in a violently polemical way, since it condemns them to appear as nothing other than traitors to their own profession. Such is the transformational violence of Koolhaas when he attempts to unmask the architects:

'Now we are left with a world without urbanism, only architecture, ever more architecture. The neatness of architecture is its seduction; it defines, excludes, limits, separates from the "rest" – but it also con-sumes. It exploits and exhausts the potentials that can be generated finally only by urbanism, and that only the specific imagination of urbanism can invent and renew. The death of urbanism – our refuge in the parasitic security of architecture – creates an immanent disaster: more and more substance is grafted on starving roots.'[1]

The relationship between architecture and urbanism seems to be of this nature: urbanism creates a possibility that architecture fulfills, but by exhausting it. What is more, this limit and sense of exhaustion have the effect of placing the architect in a very special relation to chaos.

1. Rem Koolhaas, 'What Ever Happened to Urbanism' in: *S,M,L,XL,* New York/Rotterdam, 1995.

The Sky's the Limit

This text was previously published in The New York Review of Books, *Volume 43, Number 19, November 28, 1996, as a review of* S,M,L,XL *by Rem Koolhaas and Bruce Mau, New York/Rotterdam, 1995.*

Ian Buruma

Never trust an architect. If you see one, toss a dime onto the street; he will bend over. Give him a kick, and carry on walking. GERRIT KOMRIJ, DUTCH POET

During the sixth century before Christ, King Nebuchadnezzar built a city in Babylon. It was the most fabulous city in the world, with walls thirty meters high, and terraced gardens, and temples, and, of course, the model for the biblical Tower of Babel itself, ninety-one meters in height and ninety-one meters wide, the biggest, tallest building ever made by man. By the time Herodotus saw the city, a hundred years later, it was already in ruins, conquered first by the Persians, then by troops led by Xerxes. Of the great tower he saw just the bare remains.

The Babel story has come to us as a biblical parable of hubris, of the vain attempt of human beings to act like gods and build toward Heaven. It is also a story about the diversity of languages, and the loss of comprehension, when we lose the ground under our feet and think the sky is the limit. As the Tower grew higher and higher, God turned to the Celestial Council and said: 'Come, let us go down, and there confuse their language, that they may not understand one another's speech.' In Babylon, the Tower was known as Babi-lu, the 'Gate of God'. The Jews called it Babel, which is close to *bilbul,* the Hebrew word for confusion.

Tales of architectural hubris, ending in destruction, are poignant, because they are about human folly, to be sure, but also about the power of dreams. Many dictators like to be architects, and too many architects have liked dictators. Designing the ideal city is an ancient ambition of utopian visionaries, from Plato to Le Corbusier. But visions of Heaven on earth can easily end up looking like Hell, which is why architects often are hated with a passion reserved for few other professions. We have to live in their flawed dreams. And yet their enterprise remains a source of endless fascination, because architecture, perhaps more than any other art, demonstrates both the grandeur and the fragility of human aspiration.

Rem Koolhaas, the architect, has grand ideas about how to build modern cities, and they are discussed, imitated, analysed, praised, and criticised all over the world, but he is not a utopian thinker, and he has a shrewd idea of the architect's limitations. Architecture, he said in a lecture at Rice University, 'is a dangerous profession because it is a poisonous mixture of impotence and omnipotence, in the sense that the architect almost invariably harbours megalomaniacal dreams that depend upon others, and upon circumstances, to impose and to realise … '.[1]

Yet there is more than a whiff of Babylon about Koolhaas and his work. He is so deliberately peripatetic, commuting between Europe, East Asia, and the U.S., sometimes in the space of one week, so utterly borderless, so fiercely suspicious of native identity, that he is almost a caricature of cosmopolitan hubris. As an architect, he is fascinated not by Paris, Rome, or Amsterdam, but by Manhattan, Tokyo, and Singapore. He has become obsessed by the notion of bigness, of Extra Large. Sheer size, he believes, creates Babylonian complexities that no architect can hope to control, and that is precisely the beauty of it; skyscrapers and other outsized buildings contain so much human activity that they become autonomous cities in themselves. Confusion, in a way, is an asset. Koolhaas is an aficionado of 'Babel-like multilevel car parks', 'proto-atriums', and 'mixed-use towers'.

His latest book, which, like his earlier *Delirious New York: A Retroactive Manifesto for Manhattan*,[2] is fast acquiring cult status, is a Tower of Babel of a book: thicker than a Bible (Old and New Testaments), heavier than a dictionary, denser with signs, meanings, texts, and images than Times Square. As he put it to me, over a nice cup of English tea in his quiet, uncluttered apartment on a genteel Victorian street in North London: 'It is the kind of book you cannot really produce any more. Yet we produced it'.

'We' includes the Canadian designer Bruce Mau, whose contribution is visible on every page, since this is a designed as much as a written book. And credit is also given to OMA, Koolhaas's office based in Rotterdam. OMA stands for Office for Metropolitan Architecture, which is, in the author's own opinion, 'a very pretentious name, compared to which almost any realisation may be found wanting'.[3] This is typical of Koolhaas. He has the modesty to be aware of his own megalomania. *S,M,L,XL* is a perfect example of his theory of bigness. 'Beyond a certain critical mass', he writes, 'a building becomes a Big Building. Such a mass can no longer be controlled by a single architectural gesture, or even by any combination of architectural gestures. This impossibility triggers the autonomy of its parts, but that is not the same as fragmentation: the parts remain committed to the whole'.
The book is made up of many autonomous parts: autobiographical

1. *Rem Koolhaas: Conversations with Students,* Houston/New York 1996, p. 12.
2. *Delirious New York* was originally published by Oxford University Press in 1978, and reissued by Monacelli Press in 1994.
3. *Conversations with Students,* p. 12.

sketches, architectural plans, some built, many abandoned, philosophical asides, historical anecdotes, photographs, cartoons, city maps, and a kind of personal lexicon in the margins consisting of random jottings such as (I choose at random): 'GLOBAL: I think of myself being global. I see myself participating in global activities: sitting in jets, talking to machines, eating small geometric food, and voting over the phone.'

It is an absurdly grandiose piece of work. But it is also one of the wittiest, most original, stimulating documents I have read on any subject for a long time. For the parts do form a whole. Koolhaas is one of the few architects who can write about architectural theory lucidly, with a sense of humour. Some of his ideas may be wildly over the top, but they make you think again, about cities, politics, art, and culture. Koolhaas is important, because he has come up with a bold defence of modern architecture at a time when architecture is often timid, defensive, even reactionary – at least in Europe. His enthusiasm takes you to some unexpected places: Atlanta, Fukuoka, Singapore, cities where they still build as if there is no tomorrow – or yesterday.

Rem Koolhaas was born in 1944 in Rotterdam, the eldest son of a famous Dutch writer called Anton Koolhaas. From 1952 to 1956, he lived in Indonesia, which he thinks might have given him a taste for Asian city life. He graduated from high school in Amsterdam, worked as a journalist, made experimental films, wrote scripts in Hollywood, studied architecture in London and New York, taught at Columbia and UCLA, and made his name writing *Delirious New York*. This was followed by competitions and commissions in the Netherlands, and later in France, Switzerland, Belgium, Germany, and Japan. OMA was founded in 1975, and influenced a generation of Dutch architects. The typical school of OMA building has a curved roof, sloping floors, and the look of an elegantly designed industrial plant. Typical school of OMA people are steeped in Koolhaas's ideas, and even diction. I got a taste of this at the OMA office in Rotterdam, when I asked a member of the staff if the common use of cheap industrial materials was based on aesthetic or economic considerations. The man sighed, in the way Marxists used to sigh when confronted by people who were yet to see the light. 'We don't use the word aesthetic', he said. 'It is a question of program and utilisation.' Oh, I said.

Holland is not a country that inspires people to think big. Dutch architecture, old and new, is notable for its lack of Babylonian pretensions. Unlike the British in India, the Dutch left no monumental buildings in their colonies either. There is a Dutch phrase, often quoted to sum up the national attitude toward art and life: 'If you behave normally, you are quite mad enough.' Modern Dutch architecture can be elegant, but is rarely mad, or indeed extra large. The greatest twentieth-century architects, such as Berlage, Oud, or Rietveld, shared Mondrian's genius for compact, rational design; no Lutyens-like frivolity, no Gaudí-like fantasy, no Sullivan-like towers, but clean grids, modest dimensions, and straight lines. Most of Koolhaas's Dutch work, despite his fondness for sloping roofs and floors, still echoes this tradition.

His low-income housing project in the north of Amsterdam, completed in the 1980s, is a model of Dutch sobriety. Built on a former dock site, with a view of the harbour, the IJ-plein project consists of rows of five-floor apartment blocks, a school, a supermarket, and various other neighbourhood facilities, separated by a strip of lawn from another series of slightly taller dwellings. It is an early work, done cheaply, but there are already typical Koolhaas touches. What looks at first sight like a set of dull housing blocks, and a stretch of grass, is actually a small self-contained neighbourhood. School, shops, playgrounds, lawns, and streets are woven together in such a way as to encourage social life. What could have been a suburb is something more like an autonomous town. And

although it was built only a decade ago, it has the atmosphere of an old
Amsterdam district: neighbours chat outside their doors, children play
soccer in the street, and so on. No architect can design atmosphere; it is
made by the people who live in it. But Koolhaas's project has the scale
and flexibility that allow them to do so. It is an early indication of
Koolhaas's interest in cities rather than just buildings.

The odd thing, given his theoretical predilection, is that Koolhaas has
yet to build a skyscraper.[4] But he can be very good on a small scale. He
has just finished designing a tiny gallery in New York (Lehmann Maupin
on Greene Street) – his first completed project in the U.S. Also this year
he designed a public lavatory in the Netherlands, with splendid Delft-
blue photographs on the walls – 'the most expensive toilet in Holland'.
In 1988, he built a house for friends in Rotterdam. The photographs in
S,M,L,XL show a steel and glass box, with glass walls and sliding doors
divided in panels of clean, straight lines, much like a three-dimensional
Mondrian grid. But there is something strange about this house, something more Japanese than Dutch. In the middle of the house is a patio
with mobile walls, which can be rearranged or disappear altogether, like
the paper sliding doors of a traditional Japanese house. And the floor of
the patio, above a gym, is made of glass. The effect is one of flexibility
and transparency, a feature of many Koolhaas buildings, S, M, L, or XL.
The other effect of the flexible, translucent patio is that you can feel both
inside and outside. The border between dwelling and nature is deliberately blurred.

   But there is more to Koolhaas's fondness for turning the outside in
than a taste for *japonaiserie*. I think it offers the key to his architectural
vision. Like some other contemporary architects, such as Frank Gehry
and Philippe Starck, he has revived Surrealism. When I visited the
Kunsthal, Koolhaas's arts centre in Rotterdam, completed in 1992, there

happened to be a show there of Surrealist art. One of the works was Magritte's famous painting of a painting of a brick wall, hung on an identical brick wall (*La seignée*, 1939). Another was Delvaux's picture of a nocturnal city (*La ville rouge*, 1930), made up of oddly tilted perspectives and a disconcerting clash of materials: marble, brick, and terra cotta.

I took another look at Koolhaas's curved ceilings and sloping floors, and at his use of corrugated iron and Italian marble and industrial plastic, and at the hollow tree trunks inside, and the garden laid out on a steel ramp outside, and the clouds painted on one ceiling, and the sculptured camel on the roof, and the river of stones in the garden, leading to a pond of flowers. Behind the simple, rational facade of the Kunsthal lies a hint of madness, of subversive bizarrerie. You might not like the cheap materials and the deliberately shabby finish. You might resent having to cross a raised floor of meshed steel, which could seriously injure a woman in high heels and cause bits of dirt to drop onto the people walking below. But you cannot be indifferent. Like a Luna Park, or indeed a city, the Kunsthal shocks and jolts. That is precisely the point.

In *Delirious New York* Koolhaas uses Coney Island to explain the origin of 'Manhattanism', the delirium of modern urban life. The architects of Coney Island – Tilyou, Thompson, and Reynolds – 'invented and established an urbanism based on the new Technology of the Fantastic: a permanent conspiracy against the realities of the external world'.[5] That is Koolhaas's vision of the modern city. It is why he loves New York, Los Angeles, and especially Tokyo. It is what he built on a medium scale in Rotterdam, and is now working out on a huge scale in Hollywood, where he is designing the new headquarters for MCA at Universal City, with a theme park, company housing, restaurants, a gigantic car park, and a

---

4. Koolhaas is currently working on a truly Babylonian project in Bangkok: a kind of city in the sky called Hyper Building, which will take a century to build.

5. *Delirious New York*, pp. 61-62.

stacked tower of entertainment venues, which he likens to the Tower of Babel. He speaks gleefully about the fake studio street there called City Walk. This street is now a popular playground for young people, who go there to hang out. A movie-set street turned into a part of the city: it has a surrealist ring.

It all seems a long way from rational, Calvinist Holland. Magritte and Delvaux were of course Belgian, not Dutch. But there is an element of Dutchness to which Koolhaas feels attracted. The Japanese, with their rock gardens and their dwarf trees, may be the miniaturist masters of artificial nature, but the Dutch have created nature on an extra-large scale. Much of the west coast of Holland is artificial, claimed by man from the sea. The sea was always an ambiguous adversary: it promised adventure, the chance to sail away and discover the world, but it was also liable to sweep entire towns away in a night, as it last did during the great flood of 1953. It gave people a sense of impermanence. At any moment you might have to start building all over again. One of the marginal entries in *S,M,L,XL* reads:

> DUTCHNESS: To its first generation of patriotic eulogists, Dutchness was often equated with the transformation, under divine guidance, of catastrophe into good fortune, infirmity into strength, water into dry land, mud into gold.

But now that the dikes have been finally closed, and the sea, one hopes, conquered forever, the Dutch may have lost their appetite for transformation. They are more interested in conserving what they have: postcard-pretty villages, flat green fields, old market towns, and the architectural wonder of Amsterdam – choked by traffic and covered in graffiti, but a wonder nonetheless. After decades of building hideous suburbs of concrete slabs, Dutch planners are more careful about 'context'. Grand projects are subject to revision by local politics, conservationism, claims of traditional authenticity, and financial thrift. Koolhaas hates the official suspicion of freeways and car parks and high-speed trains. He prefers streets 'with moving cars, honking horns, people crossing at traffic lights, even pushing through' to the deadly hush of pedestrian zones.

This kind of urban delirium is never planned, however, or designed, but typical of chaotic old cities. Koolhaas wants Dutch planners to build a new metropolis in the west or south of Holland, turning the old historic cities into a peripheral circle around the new capital, 'like a chain of touristic jewels'. You wonder how much spontaneous urban chaos would survive in these touristic jewels, and how delirious the new metropolis would be. Elsewhere, as we shall see, Koolhaas expresses doubt that in future cities there will be any street life at all.

Koolhaas has a way with words, which includes a facility for obscuring difficult questions by enveloping them in rather glib statements. He finds it 'crucial that the tradition of reinvention, which may be the most fertile, progressive Dutch tradition, is itself reinvented'. Sounds good. But what precisely does he mean? What is to be reinvented? You cannot reinvent chaos or spontaneity. But you can give it scope, by an architecture that doesn't pretend to offer any lasting solutions but allows people to use it in any way they like. That seems to be Koolhaas's point about bigness. Holland is, at any rate, hopelessly unsuited for the extra large. It is in every sense a small country. So Koolhaas has followed another Dutch tradition. He continues to do what Dutchmen impatient with the cramped context of their nation have done for centuries. He crosses the ocean for adventure. That is how New York was founded. It is how he founded it again.

If Manhattan hadn't existed, Koolhaas would have had to invent it, so perfectly does the combination of grid and fantasy, bigness and surrealism, business and the bizarre, fit into his urban ideal. Because of its naturally limited space, Manhattan has had to reinvent itself over and over, but its urban dynamism has to fit the geometric pattern of the grid. (Perhaps that is why Mondrian felt so at home in New York.) And by growing higher and higher, the outside of New York buildings could no longer reflect the varied activities they contained. Towers in fancy dress of neo-this or neo-that concealed hives of work and play. As Koolhaas put it in *Delirious New York,* each building 'strives to be "a City within a City"'. But instead of uniformity, this 'truculent ambition makes the Metropolis a collection of architectural city-states, all potentially at war with each other'.

What Koolhaas celebrated in his first book was not some fixed identity of Manhattan, such as, for example, the skyline, but the sheer density of human activity inside the Cities within the City. He saw Coney Island as the genesis of this, not just because of its fantastical nature (the Midget City, Dreamland, the Hanging Gardens of Babylon), but because pre-war Manhattan, like the amusement park, was driven by commercial hedonism, by hard-headed businessmen manipulated by adventurous architects in a crazy marketplace. Koolhaas's heroes are such architects as Raymond Hood (McGraw-Hill Building, 1931), who understood that, in Koolhaas's words, 'Manhattanism is the only program where the efficiency intersects with the sublime'.

For a man who likes to dismiss context, and boost the idea of permanent reinvention, Koolhaas is an imaginative and passionate historian. He cherishes history, but in an unconventional manner. He is interested in precisely the things most people reject, such as the mistakes of our fathers. As a student he did a study of the Berlin Wall, and found it of architectural interest, because of the human dramas it spawned and its sheer diversity as it snaked through urban jungles and pastoral fields. His own style was influenced by the now unfashionable modernism of the 1950s and '60s. He once wrote:

An architectural doctrine is adopted to be inevitably replaced, a few years later, by the opposite doctrine: a negative sequence in which each generation can do nothing but ridicule the preceding one. The effect of this succession of yes-no-yes is anti-historical, because it reduces architectural discourse to an incomprehensible string of disjointed phrases.[6]

One of the most arresting historical ideas in *Delirious New York* is the reversal of modernist values in pre-war and post-war Manhattan. To put it crudely, modernism was a dogma to pre-war European architects but a business opportunity to Americans. While the likes of Raymond Hood were creating their Babylonian pleasure domes in New York City, Europeans like Le Corbusier were taking modernism beyond the pleasure principle into a zone of pure rationalism. Le Corbusier thought Manhattan was not modern enough; he saw the skyscrapers in their Gothic, Renaissance, Tuscan, Beaux-Arts, Art Nouveau, Tudor fancy dress as adolescent fantasies. Typically, Koolhaas cites Salvador Dali as one European who understood the poetry of New York.

After the war, however, the combination of efficiency and delirium that made Manhattan unique had disappeared. The architectural visionaries who had got the businessmen to pay for their dreams had left no dogma or ideology. So European rationalism took over and the curtain walls of cheap skyscrapers went up with a ruthless disregard for the sublime. In the words of Koolhaas: 'The postwar architecture is the accountants' revenge on the prewar businessmen's dreams.'[7] So what was a poor Dutch architect to do? He headed east, to that far continent where Dutchmen have turned before to escape from the European context and follow their dreams of adventure.

---

6. Jacques Lucan, *OMA/Rem Koolhaas: Architecture 1970-1990*, New York 1991, p. 36.
7. *Delirious New York*, p. 285.

Koolhaas designed his first Asian building in Fukuoka, in south-western Japan, in 1991. It is a beautifully conceived block of integrated court-yard houses which, to judge from the photographs, looks more Chinese than Japanese, from the outside at any rate. According to Koolhaas it was inspired by the layout of ancient Roman towns, as well as by experiments by Mies van der Rohe. Their design is that typical Koolhaas combina-tion of intimacy and flexibility. Courtyards, grass-covered roofs, and huge windows give the houses a sense of space and of nature blending with the building. If you like stark, clean, modern design (which is in the Japanese tradition) you would want to live in them.

Visiting Japan, Koolhaas was struck by 'the vastness and shameless-ness of its ugliness'. Most Europeans share that reaction. But unlike many Europeans, Koolhaas saw merit in it, just as he saw possibilities in the Berlin Wall. For it is its juxtaposition with ugliness that makes beauty, or as he prefers it, 'the sublime', so stunning. In a way, modern Japan fol-lows Koolhaas's surrealist principle of mixing kitsch with beauty, shod-diness with fine finish, sophistication with banality, cheapness with lux-ury. It shocks and jolts.

To immerse oneself in a Japanese city, with its motels modelled after Disneyland castles, its underground shopping malls filled with fountains and artificial birdsong, its giant video screens on top of office buildings showing commercials with samurai selling rice wine or personal com-puters, its chrome and glass high-rises built around bonsai gardens, its German beer halls and Zen temples, can be a surreal experience. A pop-ular tourist destination near Nagasaki consists of a newly built 'old' Dutch town, constructed around a replica of the royal palace in The Hague, complete with an eighteenth-century Dutch garden which never existed in Holland itself. It is a theme park meant for people to visit, and live in. You can see why Koolhaas is fascinated by Japan. Context has become meaningless. Apart from a few neighbourhoods in Kyoto and

Nara, traditional authenticity, in the sense of conserved antiquity, which Europeans prize so highly in their own historic cities, is almost entirely absent in Japan, or indeed anywhere in East Asia. Japanese have had to rebuild their urban environment, because after 1945 there was virtually nothing left of the old.

And yet I should think the Nagasaki 'Dutch' village is precisely the kind of city planning Koolhaas would argue against, for it is an attempt to create a phoney context, based on a phoney tradition. The fake Dutch houses and the bungalow suburbs built around the theme park have not attracted many Japanese who actually want to live there. The point is not that the fake tradition is Dutch and not Japanese, but that a model town is the opposite of a truly urban environment. (So is that studio street in Hollywood, but then nobody lives there.) The phoney village is in complete contrast to the big, ugly, urban jungles, such as Tokyo, Osaka, or Fukuoka, which Japanese have managed to make so supremely liveable.

Even when cities were not destroyed by fire, earthquakes, or war, Chinese, Japanese, and Koreans have been remarkably sanguine about tearing down old buildings and building new ones. Old Singapore has virtually disappeared, old Shanghai and Peking are swiftly disappearing. This is partly a question of commercial greed, partly of expediency, and partly of habit. Chinese culture was passed on through its literature, not architectural monuments. Cities were not built to last forever. Japanese cities of paper, bamboo, and wood could not possibly have done so. Now the same combination of commercialised fantasy, business sense, and technological efficiency that went into pre-war 'Manhattanism' is at work in East Asia. And just as people in the West were busily condemning post-war modernism as a failed experiment, Asian architects, consumers, and developers were embracing it with gusto. Cheap, high-rise buildings are sprouting like forests from Singapore to Seoul.

Koolhaas writes well on Singapore, which he takes as seriously as he once took Manhattan. He subjected Singapore to the same quasi-archeological analysis. And he came up with Singapore as the model for what he sees as the 'Generic City' of the future: a city divorced from context, based on nothing but efficiency, with history reduced to a token theme park (in the case of Singapore, a recreated Chinatown), a city of hotels and shopping malls, with nature represented by golf courses or simulated by indoor gardens in air-conditioned atriums. To a self-confessed global man, addicted to jetting around the world, the idea of a city based on speed, efficiency, and mobility, a city built like a giant airport, a megalopolis of atriums and multi-story car parks, might seem like a kind of Utopia. But there is something nightmarish about it too.

Koolhaas knows that, but he is not so much interested in judging Singapore as in understanding it. He wants to deal with the modern world as he finds it. He is not a Utopian architect with a political vision of the ideal city, or society. He doesn't think architects are capable of building ideal cities anyway, any more than politicians can build ideal societies. Koolhaas, in one of his typical metaphors, likes to think of himself as a surfer on the waves of history. 'The force and the direction of the wave are uncontrollable, it breaks, the surfer can only, in exploiting it, "master" it by choosing his route'.[8] His scepticism about the predictability of the future is commendable, but anti-utopianism has its limits too. For a refusal to make political judgments puts one at the mercy of the strongest, whose intentions are not necessarily benign.

I am not especially keen on Singapore myself. But I can see why modern public housing, shopping malls, and office towers seem to be less alienating there than in Europe. (The U.S., I suppose, lies somewhere between Asia and Europe in this respect.) The sheer density of Asian city life, the crowds, the hurly-burly of non-stop shopping make new city

8. Lucan, *OMA/Rem Koolhaas*, p. 37.

centres in Asia more tolerable than over-regulated, placid European urban malls. Singaporeans, like other East Asians, are almost all newly rich, and have barely emerged from colonial humiliation. Modernity to them means power and wealth; traditional houses on stilts, old shop-houses, and all the other physical remnants of an older way of life mean poverty and backwardness. Western tourists and a few Asian intellectuals might regret the destruction of the old context and identity, but most people have other things on their minds. And given a certain amount of freedom, Asians are quite capable of creating their own context, which is why the Generic City doesn't really exist: Tokyo doesn't look like Singapore, or Bangkok like Hong Kong, despite the common liking for chrome, glass, plastic, and pizza parlours.

There is, however, another side to the wholesale modernisation of Asian cities, which Koolhaas touches upon, without dwelling on it. This is the matter of coercion. 'The Generic City', he writes, 'has a (sometimes distant) relationship with a more or less authoritarian regime'. This is clearly true. The radical transformation of Singapore – 'a test bed of the tabula rasa', as Koolhaas calls it – would not have been possible without an authoritarian regime. Nor is the current destruction and construction of, say, Shanghai possible without coercion.

The results can be disturbing. Poor people living in the more or less squalid conditions of central-city districts may not care much about authenticity, or fret about their identity, but there is a context from which most of them don't want to be liberated: the neighbourhood, where they can walk to the shops, chat with the neighbours, drink at the corner cafe. It is not just sentimental to deplore the way people in Chinese cities are bussed away to distant suburbs so that corporate buildings can be built on the sites of their former homes.

Soon only the rich will be able to afford to live in central Shanghai, Hong Kong, Singapore, or Tokyo. Koolhaas's prediction that 'the street' in the Generic City 'is dead' may turn out to be right. He says this without regret or approval, and notes that public space will be located more on our cybernetic superhighways and TV screens than in our city squares. Perhaps. But if he is serious about reinventing urban life, he will have to address political questions, as well as technological ones. Surfing is not always good enough.[9]

There always has existed a devil's pact between architects and dictators to carry out radical projects. In fifteenth-century Italy great chunks of old cities were destroyed by military engineers and despotic princes. Their thinking was not so different from that of Lee Kuan Yew and his architects: modern efficiency and social control were the thing. Baron Haussmann's razing of old Paris to make way for wide boulevards and other grand projects was done in the same spirit. Of course, much of what we think of today as typically Parisian – the Paris identity, so to speak – is the result of Haussmann's radicalism. To create new cities, Generic or otherwise, you often need coercive power on your side. These days that means corporations more often than princes, but the methods used are not always less harsh. A popular way to remove inhabitants from their old homes in Tokyo during the 1980s, when the corporate building boom was at its height, was to hire gangsters. First the thugs would offer money, then threaten to use force, and then, if that didn't work, use it. The buildings went up, and up, until the bubble burst, and the developers went bankrupt.

Koolhaas cannot be blamed for such practices. Nor does he advocate the destruction of old cities. But it is well to be aware of the temptations of coercive power, when you hear an architect expanding on the fasci-

9. Koolhaas is more critical in practice than in theory. He said in an interview that he had turned down many projects in China, because he did not approve of the crude destruction and construction boom taking place there. This interview appeared in the Spanish journal *El Croquis*, No. 79 (1996).

nation of the tabula rasa. It is also easy to imagine the temptation for a European, bored and stymied by the constraints of the Old World, to see the U.S. and Asia as great tabulae rasae. I asked a colleague of Koolhaas's at the OMA office in Rotterdam about Koolhaas's ideas on building a new capital city in Holland. And I was told that Holland was much too democratic for such a plan to succeed. Too many interests have to be taken into account, too many voices heard.

There is, I think, an element of hyperbole in Koolhaas's visions anyway. His theory of the Generic City is a polemic against European cultural conservatism. In fact, his description of Singapore is not without ambivalence. He admires the boldness of building a brand-new city, but describes the result as a 'Potemkin metropolis'. This air of unreality, of a 'city without qualities', is a universal problem of modern architecture. It may be liberating, but when modernism is reduced to pure rationalism, it is the liberation of death. As Koolhaas himself admits:

> We can make things, but not necessarily make them real. Singapore represents the point where the volume of the new overwhelms the volume of the old, has become too big to be animated by it, has not yet developed its own vitality. Mathematically, the third millennium will be an experiment in this form of soullessness. ...

What Koolhaas is advocating, then, it seems to me, is not the destruction of old cities to replace them with clusters of hotels and shopping malls. His argument is that old city centres will become unliveable, if they are not revitalised by the shock of the new. The double act of making a fetish of the identity of old cities while adapting them to modern life puts them under intolerable strain, for there is only so much you can do to make an old city new while disguising that you are doing so. Besides, it has the perverse effect of robbing them of authenticity, of making them into fake antiques. In Amsterdam, for example, more and more houses are being demolished, except for the old facades, which are grafted onto new buildings like masks. And the sprawling peripheries of old cities are denied an urban identity because they remain just that: the despised environs of the historic metropolis, which alone represents 'the city'.

That explains Koolhaas's vision of a new Dutch metropolis. Making the old city centres peripheral, you take the load off them and allow them to breathe. At the same time new architecture should be less apologetic, more bold in its modernity, in a word, more urban. Koolhaas is content to leave old cities alone. He is stimulated by the wastelands of cities, the neglected industrial zones, bombed tabulae rasae, and derelict suburban blocks. That is why he likes Rotterdam more than Amsterdam, and London or Berlin more than Paris. Bomb sites can be turned into new cities. Dereliction can be made beautiful. His most interesting project to date can be seen in what was one of the most wasted, peripheral cities in France: Lille.

Until recently, Lille was a melancholy dump. The textile and mining industries that once made it prosperous had collapsed, and two World Wars left horrible scars. The old city, *vieux Lille,* was a dilapidated, crumbling wreck of a place, too depressed to be romantic. Lille was a town to avoid. Then the keen French and the more reluctant British finally completed the cross-channel tunnel, or Chunnel, closing the gap between the Continent and Britain. This opened up endless possibilities, especially for an architect who likes to think of space in terms of transportation: air miles, rail links, freeways. If the tracks of the TGV (super-fast train) from London to Paris to Brussels could go through Lille, the geography of the city would change. No longer just an urban dump in France Nord, Lille would be little more than an hour away from Paris and London, a European hub of constant movement.

The city government of Lille managed, through some deft political footwork, to get the TGV route, and Koolhaas was given his first extra-large project in 1989: the master plan for turning one million square metres within walking distance of old Lille into a complex of hotels, restaurants, department stores, offices, parking garages, a congress centre (Congrexpo), and a new railway station. It was called Euralille. Only in France, with its tradition of strong government, would a politician – in this case, Pierre Mauroy, mayor of Lille and former French prime minister – have had the wherewithal to push such a scheme through. Koolhaas himself designed Congrexpo, which resembles a space-age football stadium, a huge oblong building that contains a network of halls, car parks, and other public spaces. Jean Nouvel designed the commercial centre. The station was designed by Jean-Marie Duthilleul. The office tower built on top of the railway tracks in the shape of a giant armchair is by Christian de Portzamparc, and Marie and François Delhay did the hotel.

On a walk through Euralille I came across a large group of Japanese architects, taking notes and gawking at the shopping centres, car parks, movable station roofs, office complexes, and walkways with the excitement of provincials in the big city. They were from Tokyo. And this was Lille! The astonishing thing about Euralille, and this is really the point, is how this modern development, including of course the TGV itself, has revived old Lille. Nobody lives in Euralille. It is a place to work, eat, buy, or stay overnight, a transitional city, full of commercial activity, but no neighbourhoods. Old Lille, however, is now a thriving area of fine, renovated houses, excellent restaurants, attractive, well-stocked shops, and also of squares and streets teeming with life. A bold, big, modern architectural development has revitalised a dying old city. And new Euralille didn't even have to be ugly to show off the beauty of old Lille. What is striking about Euralille is not its bigness, but the intricacy and complexity of its design. The different, autonomous parts are so intertwined that the whole looks magnificent in the vast, webbed, human way of a Gothic cathedral.

Beauty is perhaps the best-kept secret of this Dutch architect, who claims to feel most at home on airplanes or in anonymous modern hotels. Sitting comfortably in his elegant London flat, he told me a story about a Japanese photographer he admires, called Araki Nobuyoshi. Araki's photographs of nude girls tied up in cheap motels, or of Tokyo streets, cluttered with the plastic rubble of modernity, are taken in a deliberately throwaway style, as if they were snapshots by an obsessive amateur. Many are technically crude, purposely vulgar. But Araki has a secret, which only a few people are allowed to share: a hidden collection of beautifully made, technically polished, exquisite photographs. Araki, said Koolhaas, can make a garbage bag look beautiful. The same could be said of Koolhaas himself.

Net population change per hour

+20
Los Angeles

0 −2 −1
Chicago Philadelphia
Detroit

0
London

−3
Madrid

+31
Mexico City

+18
Lima

+
La

+33
Sao Paolo

−5
Moscow
et

+28
Istanbul

−2
Seoul

+15
0 Tokyo
Osaka

+33
Karachi

+48
Delhi

+25
Calcutta

+67
Dhaka

3

+43
Bombay

+17
Bangkok

+23
Manila

+38
Jakarta

METHOD

Neil Leach
Anthony Vidler
Okwui Enwezor
Fredric Jameson
Matthew Stadler
René Boomkens

C<AMO>UFLAGE

Neil Leach

How are we to understand the role of aesthetics in the work of Rem Koolhaas? It is clear that his published work subscribes to a highly visual logic, where painterly writings are inserted within a seamless landscape of imagery and text. Koolhaas is a contemporary Baudelairean 'painter of modern life'. This emphasis on the visual could be seen as not only the strength but also the potential weakness in Koolhaas's methodology. On the one hand, it allows him to articulate with considerable graphic clarity the complex structures of society, but on the other hand it precisely traps him within the realm of the visual, and exposes him to charges of aestheticisation. The products are admittedly seductive, exquisitely designed visual objects. But are we then to accuse Koolhaas of turning the world into an anaestheticised domain of coffee table images and neat sound-bites?

The question is particularly apposite in the context of Koolhaas's study on Lagos. Here one of the world's most troubled cities is analysed through what has become a consistent methodological approach. Lagos may seem like 'hell on earth', a dysfunctional, chaotic city, but once it is subjected to the penetrating gaze of the AMO research machinery, a different city emerges, one in which complex processes of filtering, sorting and redistribution come into play. It is as though out of the complexity of Lagos certain self-organising patterns begin to emerge. Lagos, it would seem, is not so bad after all. This, in itself, is controversial enough. To be sure, many who have experienced Lagos, and who know it well, would criticise the project for being too optimistic. For many Lagos cannot be redeemed. It remains 'hell on earth', and no matter how ingenious the self-organising mechanisms that have been brought into play – mechanisms that, at best, merely serve to alleviate slightly a profoundly problematic situation – Lagos is still a troubled city.

The question that arises, however, is not so much whether the AMO view is correct, but whether there is something in the presentation that undermines the entire project. From the position of critics such as Jean Baudrillard, such studies amount to a form of aestheticisation. They turn the world into an escapist, rose-tinted version of itself.[1]

The problem lies, then, in the very packaging of the project, the elegant, design-conscious presentation of Lagos in a Bruce Mau inspired product, that can be found for sale in all the bookshops of chic art galleries throughout the world alongside Aldo Rossi espresso makers and Philippe Starck lemon squeezers. Has Koolhaas turned Lagos into a bijou designer object? Has Koolhaas anaesthetised Lagos?

Here I wish to argue that to dismiss Koolhaas in this way would be

---

1. To quote from my own work: 'The aestheticization of the world induces a form of numbness. It reduces any notion of pain to the level of the seductive image. What is at risk in this process of aestheticization is that political and social content may be subsumed, absorbed and denied. The seduction of the image works against any underlying sense of social commitment. Architecture is potentially compromised within this aestheticized realm. Architects, it would seem, are particularly susceptible to an aesthetic which fetishises the ephemeral image, the surface membrane. The world becomes aestheticized and anaesthetized. In the intoxicating world of the image, the aesthetics of architecture threaten to become the anaesthetics of architecture.' Neil Leach, *The Anaesthetics of Architecture,* Cambridge, Mass 1999, p. 45.

to miss the subtleties in his approach. Many of the critiques made about aestheticisation within a culture of postmodernity need to be revisited. Indeed the conditions of postmodernity have themselves been transcended, as cultural production has evolved in response to changing material conditions. A new paradigm has emerged which engages more knowingly with the rich, visual terrain of contemporary culture.

I wish to present a theory of 'camouflage', which will allow us to judge Koolhaas in a more sympathetic light, and to understand the significance of design in both his written output and his architecture. This theory is presented as a retroactive manifesto for the visual logic within Koolhaas's work that reveals the social role of design in his polemical stance against the junk spaces of our contemporary cultural horizon.

But why should any retroactive manifesto be necessary? One reason is that it serves to articulate concerns implicit within the work which are otherwise unaddressed. Among those concerns the question of aesthetics is primary. Most would agree on the elegance of his buildings, but Koolhaas himself makes few references to aesthetic considerations. In this, Koolhaas subscribes to a trait all too common in contemporary architectural circles. The work may be beautiful, but its beauty is never acknowledged. It is as though 'aesthetics' has become a dirty word in contemporary design culture.

The issue comes into focus when Koolhaas's published work is taken into account. What seems to characterise his many studies undertaken under the auspices of either AMO or the Graduate School of Design at Harvard, is that they are all attempts to understand the workings of contemporary culture. Through graphs, diagrams and other forms of statistical analysis, they explore the factors that inform and influence society today. Their emphasis is on the processes that lie beneath the surface level manifestations.[2] What is curious, however, about these publications is that they are always elegantly presented and carefully designed. Although the primary concern is an attempt to understand process they nonetheless subscribe to an unacknowledged discourse of representation. These are not just diagrams and graphs. They are exquisitely designed diagrams and graphs. Koolhaas's collaborations with designers such as Bruce Mau reveal that design is a crucial concern for him.

Representation – the realm of aesthetics – has become the repressed discourse in Koolhaas's works, whether books or buildings.[3] Yet it is not as though Koolhaas completely ignores aesthetics. For what is his polemic against 'junkspace' but an aesthetic crusade? The paradox, however, is that there is no theory of aesthetics to accompany Koolhaas's theory of junk – there is no gospel of beauty to go alongside the 'new gospel of ugliness'. This article is therefore an attempt to supply the missing theory of aesthetics in Koolhaas's work.

Forget Baudrillard

In recent years we have begun to see various visual strategies emerging in response to an image driven culture. These strategies have evolved as a knowing manipulation of the use of images, whose early antecedents include the work of the photographer, Cindy Sherman, but whose more recent articulations can be found in designer journals such as *Wallpaper**, but also throughout popular culture. I wish to argue that it is precisely in this realm that we can locate works such as *S,M,L,XL*.

2. These studies therefore fit broadly within a methodological approach common in contemporary architectural culture, inspired by the thinking of Gilles Deleuze, where strategically process is privileged over representation.
3. This reflects a broader tendency through much of architectural culture which can be read as an attempt to move beyond the scenography of postmodern culture. We should recognise, however, that, in Deleuze's terms, process is always linked to representation. Process folds into representation, and vice versa. Strategically, there may be a need to emphasise process over representation, but the significance of representation should not be overlooked.
4. Guy Debord, *La société du spectacle,* Paris 1967 and 1971. English translations: *The Society of the Spectacle,* Detroit 1977, and translated by Donald Nicholson-Smith, New York 1994.
5. Jean Baudrillard, *The Perfect Crime,* translated by Chris Turner, London 1996.

Visual strategies have always existed in one form or another in human operations, but they have become dominant within our contemporary image-based culture. They amount to an overcoming of the conditions of postmodernity. The temporal specificity of this mode of operating is important. Human beings are to be recognised here as mutant creatures, who are constantly evolving, and forever devising new strategies for dealing with their ever-changing material conditions.

These new strategies come to represent an effective response to contemporary conditions, but so too one that has begun to define those conditions. Far from being a distraction from the real business of living, the visual domain has come to delineate the very horizon of contemporary existence. As such, it forces us to call into question critiques of postmodernity which adopt a predominantly negative view towards our image-conscious society.

We need to recognise that human beings are no longer overwhelmed by the onslaught of images within a highly visual culture, but see images as a domain of self-empowerment. This realm of images should be read not in negative terms as a loss or concealment of some original ideal state, but rather in positive terms as a mode of self-expression. In this respect the concept of camouflage is aligned closely with psychoanalytic perspectives which recognise the important role of representation in the constitution of identity.

As such, this new visual paradigm exposes fundamental problems in arguments by critics of postmodernity who posit that reality is somehow lost beneath the play of surface imagery within contemporary culture. It is not, as Guy Debord once maintained, that in the Society of the Spectacle identity is lost as everything is mediated through images and commodities.[4] Rather, in a culture of branding, identity is itself forged through that domain. Nor is it, as Baudrillard maintained, that reality itself has been so obscured by the 'ecstasy of communication' of our culture of hyperreality, that it has effectively been 'stolen'.[5] Rather, if we follow psychoanalytic thinking, what we take for the real is in fact the imaginary. It is precisely through the imaginary realm of representation that so-called reality is acted out.

Moreover, we can begin to see how the totalising treatment of images within much postmodern discourse is itself an impoverished one. Within the work of many critics of our image based society there seems to be a somewhat homogeneous understanding of images. No accommodation is made for design and composition. Yet an image can be effective or not at establishing some form of connectivity, and much depends on the nature of that particular image.

Simulacra, simulation, superficiality. Yet this depthless domain of hyperreality in which we live, this culture of surface effects, clearly has certain positive attributes. We need to move beyond the critiques of Debord and Baudrillard, which lead to something of an aesthetic cul-de-sac, and which leave architects and anyone else working in the visual domain radically disempowered and incapable of operating effectively. But more than this, we need to recognise the vital role that the visual domain plays within our contemporary cultural horizon.

Rather than hankering after some lost culture of depth, we should embrace our present culture as a shallow realm of the seductive and the alluring, yet one which compensates for its very shallowness by its universality of appeal. Images serve as the site of identification. They allow us to relate to the world, either in terms of the way we dress and present ourselves, or in terms of the way in which we read ourselves into the environment.

For it is not that reality has been lost beneath a world of simulation. Simulation itself has become the new realm of interaction. Tactics are therefore required that not only acknowledge this phenomenon, but also tap into it. This is already evident in the work of AMO, where as a means of supplementing meticulous data analysis, strategies such as 'Tourism' have been adopted as ways of navigating our contemporary cultural horizon, while key Baudrillardian concepts, such as simulation, have been re-appropriated and turned into productive tools.

As Jeffrey Inaba comments: 'AMO has adopted "Tourism" as a means of inquiry. To complement our investigation of "hard" facts, AMO has turned to intensive observation. Despite criticism that it is subjective and circumstantial, observation in the form of "Tourism" is an invaluable vehicle to take otherwise unattainable information from real world events. In this respect, we are willing to compromise critical detachment in exchange for the benefits of immediacy, objectivity for acute insight, and competency for acquired expertise. The concept of Tourism concedes that superficiality and adulteration are inevitable. At the same time, it announces that contamination is welcome. AMO is eager to take stock of mock realities. The more simulated the better.'[6]

The manifestations of this new visual paradigm are everywhere evident, and play a central role in the work of AMO. But how exactly are we to explain them? How do they operate? Here I would like to offer 'a theory of camouflage' as a way of trying to understand the logic behind this visual paradigm.

A Theory of Camouflage

1.0   What are we to understand by the term 'camouflage'? Let us start by clarifying that the term is being used here not within the narrow, conventional sense of military camouflage, but within the broader sense of representation and self representation that is always already at work within culture. Military camouflage is but a sub-set of a larger category

6. Jeffrey Inaba, 'Plan for Now' in: Neil Leach (ed.), *Designing for a Digital World*, London 2002, p. 139.

of camouflage. Indeed the emerging use of camouflage combat clothing within the fashion industry reveals not only that camouflage can be a kind of clothing, but also that clothing can itself be a kind of camouflage. In this respect, the flamboyant formal outfits which make soldiers stand out on military parades are as much an example of camouflage as the outfits worn during military combat which serve to hide them within their environment.

1.1   Camouflage is a form of masquerade, a mode of representation. But camouflage is not restricted to self representation in terms of clothing, make-up, hairstyle and so on. Rather camouflage operates through the medium of representation itself – through art, dance, music, poetry, architecture, and so on. Camouflage does not entail the cloaking of the self, so much as the relating of the self to the environment through the medium of representation. Aesthetic expressions of all kinds, from high art to popular music, from jewellery to urban planning, operate as a kind of mediation between the self and the environment.

1.2   Camouflage, then, is understood here as a mechanism for inscribing an individual within a given cultural setting. This need not be a literal state of visual equivalence with that setting, such that the definition of the self is lost against the background of the other. The role of camouflage is not to disguise, but to offer a medium through which to relate to the other. Camouflage constitutes a mode of symbolisation. It operates as a form of connectivity.

1.3   Military camouflage, then, offers us a very limited understanding of the possibilities of camouflage. Nonetheless, the specific connotations of military camouflage are helpful in illustrating two important attributes of camouflage, its emphasis on the domain of the visual and its strategic nature.

2.0   Camouflage is not restricted to the visual domain. It can be enacted within the domains of the other senses, especially smell and hearing. Perfume is precisely part of the masquerade of self-representation that defines the operations of camouflage. So too is music which is often used to provide an ambient setting. Yet camouflage is primarily visual, at least within the realm of human behaviour. The chameleon, a creature that has little sense of smell or hearing, but a highly developed sense of vision, is perhaps the ultimate creature of visual camouflage. Human beings have a less developed sense of vision and more advanced capacities in the other senses, but nonetheless vision remains their most effective sense. Human beings are creatures that tend to privilege vision, and visual camouflage plays a key role in their behaviour. Many animals, by comparison, have a more sophisticated sense of smell or hearing. A dog, for example, may sense smells and sounds far beyond the range detectable by humans.

2.1   Camouflage can therefore be read as an interface with the world. It operates as a masquerade that re-presents the self, just as self representation through make-up, dress, hair style, etcetera, is a form of self re-presentation. But this need not be a temporary condition. The surface masquerade may have a lasting impact on questions of identity. Far from denying any true sense of self beneath, it may actually contribute to a sense of self. Camouflage should therefore be seen as a mechanism for constituting human identity through the medium of representation.

3.0 Traditionally camouflage has been taken to refer to a strategy of concealment against a given background. It is important to recognise, however, that, within the more comprehensive understanding of the term being used here, camouflage refers to both revealing and concealing. Camouflage delineates a spectrum of degrees of definition of the self against a given background. The chameleon, after all, uses its changes in colouration both to blend into an environment on some occasions, and to stand out on others.

These changes are dependent on the mood of the chameleon. Human beings replicated this behaviour. At various moments human beings wish either to stand out from the crowd or to blend in. Camouflage therefore acts as a device for individuals to relate to a given background through the medium of representation, either by becoming part of that background, or by distinguishing themselves from it.

3.1   Here we might cite the work of more positive thinkers, such as Fredric Jameson who looks to the realm of representation for a mechanism of reinserting the individual within society. Jameson has developed a notion of 'cognitive mapping', which serves to overcome the lack of spatial co-ordinates within a society of late capitalism.[7] He sees the potential of such mapping within the aesthetic domain. What we need today, Jameson seems to be saying, is a viable form of aesthetic expression that reinserts the individual into society. The aesthetic domain can therefore be seen to be somewhat Janus-faced. It is both the source of many of our problems, in a culture in which everything is co-opted into images and commodities, and potentially the way out.

3.2   Camouflage offers a mechanism of locating the self against the otherwise homogenising placelessness of contemporary existence. It thereby promotes a sense of attachment and connection to place. Camouflage may therefore provide a sense of belonging in a society where the hegemony of traditional structures of belonging – the family, church and so on – has begun to break down. This aesthetic sense of belonging can be compared to other modes of belonging, such as religious devotion or romantic attachment.

4.0   The question remains as to what aesthetic expression these operations might take. It is clear that any such expression is governed by the conditions of the age. The aesthetic realm operates as a process of symbolisation that allows the individual to find meaning in the world. This meaning is not a question of signification, as though aesthetic expressions were to be valued only for their hidden meanings which are to be decoded. Rather meaning is produced through a dynamic interaction between the individual and aesthetic expression. Yet this meaning is context dependent, and may easily lose its relevance. Thus we find various artistic expressions that were once highly meaningful, now appearing redundant. The very example of outmoded art, which no longer holds any popular resonance, serves to illustrate how art does not escape fashion – in its broadest sense – but is precisely inscribed within a logic of fashion. Fashion determines what aesthetic expressions are relevant to a particular context.

4.1   Aesthetic production should maintain the capacity to operate as a mediation between the self and the environment, but only aesthetic production whose design has been carefully controlled can achieve this. The difference between productive and unproductive modes of expression is therefore a question of design. In this respect we can recognise the important social role of design in providing a form of connectivity for 'cognitively mapping' an individual within the environment. Design becomes a crucial consideration for the effective operation of camouflage.

Conclusion
The concept of 'Camouflage' begins to highlight the significance of design in contemporary society. Exquisitely designed works such as S,M,L,XL can therefore be interpreted not simply as highly aesthetic publications that could be accused of a process of 'glossification' – of turning the world into a designer representation of itself. Rather they can be seen to be operating in the very space of contemporary culture, a space that is highly visual.

7. Fredric Jameson, 'Cognitive Mapping' in: Michael Hardt and Kathi Weeks (eds.), *The Jameson Reader*, London 1999, pp. 277-287.

But, more than this, the concept of camouflage allows us to recognise a further social dimension to the aesthetic realm. Beyond any critiques of the anaestheticised nature of the aesthetic realm, design plays a crucial role in providing a mode of symbolisation. There is, then, another side to the argument. The analyses of AMO, with their designer graphs, maps and diagrams, their elegantly produced texts and illustrations, could indeed be accused of aestheticisation – a rinsing, in other words, of their subject matter of the social and the political – but at the same time, they operate within a new paradigm which recognises that there is a further social dimension to design in offering a form of connectivity, that allows people to relate to their environment.

As such, the concept of 'Camouflage' can also respond to some of the questions that Koolhaas himself raises. In his essay on the Generic City, for example, Koolhaas offers a critique of the placelessness of the contemporary cityscape, where each city is virtually indistinguishable from the next. The theory of camouflage, however, would seem to suggest that design itself can overcome this condition by providing a mechanism for relating the individual to the environment. Design here must be contrasted to junk. If the junk city has become the placeless generic city, the exquisitely designed city can become the city of a new form of spatial mapping. This theory of camouflage is therefore presented not only as a retroactive manifesto through which to appreciate Koolhaas's work, but also as a contribution to the debates which he initiates.

The concept of 'Camouflage' will allow us, at least, to move beyond the often simplistic denigration of the aesthetic realm within recent critiques of postmodern culture, and to grasp the complexities involved in our negotiation with the world afforded through that realm. Above all, it will allow us to recognise the important strategic significance of aesthetics in contemporary culture in general and in Rem Koolhaas's work in particular.

rony is certainly the figurative mode of the early works of OMA and
of the work that, more than any other, served to give these works a
coherent 'program' of their own: Rem Koolhaas's *Delirious New York*.
This book, with its unabashed postscript of OMA images and texts,
is equally unabashed in its choice of subject matter and formal strategies, both on which are borrowed from a long tradition of modernist
work on metropolis. In it is displayed a sophisticated knowledge of all
the techniques by which the modern city, as unconscious artefact, was
to be transformed into the self-conscious agony of the avant-garde:
the sociology and psychopathology of metropolis advanced by Georg
Simmel, Sigmund Freud, and Emile Durkheim; the technical ideology
of metropolis from Otto Wagner to Le Corbusier; and, just as important,
the mythic structure of metropolis essayed by Baudelaire in *Le Spleen
de Paris* (1855-1865) and brought to a high art of montage in the filmic
texts of Walter Benjamin.

This from the hands of Rem Koolhaas, a former filmmaker and script-
writer, was predictable. What was not was the way in which these bor-
rowings were themselves ironically subverted by the subjects treated.
For how should we laugh, for example, at the spectacle of positive
projects like that of the 'Fighting the Flames' event on Coney Island
juxtaposed to the actual fire that destroyed the fairground in 1911, a
fair created for pleasure at the expense of the masses and contrasting
with their degradation? Political irony, surrealist irony, supreme irony,
but this when juxtaposed to the future projects of pleasure and economic gain in Manhattan, exposed finally as nonironic.
On the one hand, the facts of the case, set out with bald titles - 'Foundation,' 'Fire,' 'End'; on the other, the juxtaposition – itself a time-
honoured montage technique – that throws everything, including the
stance of the author, into doubt.

This, one might think, would make excellent, dry humorous reading, but would not necessarily provide the foundations of any kind of building. It would seem that the very choice of such techniques arms the critically self-conscious writer against the fate of the avant-garde architect. We look for no Welfare Palace Hotel to be built on landfill – indeed, we hope for none; the irony would only operate if the mental rather than the physical image remains intact.

But build OMA will, and, side by side with the early studies in *Witz*, a number of serious projects have merged, for hotels, resorts, condominiums, office buildings, residences, and even prison and parliament houses. Not the stuff of irony, surely. Yet in a subtle and intriguing way, OMA has succeeded in maintaining its dominant figure, through the subjects of its new building activity. And this time it is sustained not simply by the nature of the drawing and the narrative; nor are we presented with elaborate scenarios of actions side by side with their illustration. The drawings, it is true, are exquisite, but they are in no sense the surrealistic machines of urban wit previously painted by Madelon Vriesendorp. Rather they are ruthlessly 'scientific,' the results of calculation and computer graphics. View after view, cutting through the received angle of vision simply by virtue of the flexibility of the machine. Analysis of sight lines, of massing, of the movement of people and objects takes its place beside the most accurate representation of reality available. These are no longer the transformations of formalist technique, dedicated to destroying our commonplaces by the unexpected, but more the realism of a natural vision, deployed ruthlessly to tell us how, indeed, it would look.

Terminal Modernity: Rem Koolhaas's Discourse on Entropy

Okwui Enwezor

I am an ephemeral and a not too discontented citizen of a metropolis considered modern because all known taste has been evaded in the furnishings and the exterior of the houses as well as in the layout of the city.
ARTHUR RIMBAUD [1]

Tabula Rasa: A Theory of Everything, *Apropos* the City

The city as theme and subject remains undiminished in its attraction to legions who place it at the nexus of modernity. One imagines that Paris in the nineteenth century was for Rimbaud what New York, in the twentieth century, is to Rem Koolhaas, with Manhattan as its epicenter, a vector of new sensations at a level no other city can claim. Likewise, Walter Benjamin, born at the end of the nineteenth century, would look back at the unitary urbanism of Baron Hausmann's Paris in 'Paris, Capital of the 19th Century'. Koolhaas, born in 1944, in the middle of the twentieth century, would also look back at the paroxysm of architecture in *fin de siècle* New York as the radical conclusion of organised planning and speculative urbanism in his great book *Delirious New York: A Retroactive Manifesto for Manhattan.*

The critical importance of this study of the 'greatest' city of the twentieth century to the entire *œuvre* of Koolhaas is such that every analysis of his work and practice inexorably goes back to and begins with

Delirious New York, for it is in this book that one intuits (and this has often been demonstrated) the kernel of hard truth surrounding all of his work on the city. The theories and ideas posed in the book represent Koolhaas's tabula rasa; a kind of theory of everything, *apropos* the city and urbanism for the twenty-first century. *Delirious New York,* designated by Koolhaas as a retroactive manifesto for Manhattan, however, is not a manifesto as such, but a dialectic for thinking the obsolete and the spectral: modernity as a peculiarly Western fantasy upon whose wreckage ceaselessly recur the phantoms of Utopia and catastrophe, renewal and destruction.

In this dialectic, Koolhaas's work very much identifies with the ideas of early twentieth-century avant-garde movements which embarked on the systematic dismantling of tradition. Manhattan, along with its spatial elaboration: *Manhattanism,* reveals the combinatory poetics of this creative destruction (one thinks here of Gordon Matta-Clark's idea of anarchitecture) and spatial suture, that is to say a montage of forms superimposed on the ekistic grid of spectacle and property speculation born of the nineteenth century. Spectacularly oneiric and concrete, *Manhattanism* represents, at the tail end of twentieth century modernity, the very condition of the end of the West.[2] While this interpretation is not firmly stated in Koolhaas's thesis on the skyscraper city, it registers it at every other level. For instance, as he began to examine models

1. Arthur Rimbaud, 'City' in: Louise Varèse, *Illuminations,* New York 1957, p. 57.
2. Since the apocalyptic attacks of 9/11/2001, the tussle between civilisation theorists and those of radical Islam has staked an ideological ground on the outcome of the struggle that presently engulfs the world. No doubt, for the attackers, their considered choice of the twin towers of the World Trade Center and the conflagration that it set off in downtown Manhattan, and the push to rebuild the towers by those wishing to defy the attackers, represent a new way of symbolising the city as a site of new struggle for modernity. It is to be said, that not just the Twin Towers, with their strategic location at the heart of global finance were attacked, but the very idea of the Western metropolis and its modernity were conscripted into this conflict. Nothing could be starker than to compare the image of burning Manhattan and that of Kabul during the climax of the campaign in Afghanistan.
3. Rem Koolhaas, *Delirious New York,* New York 1994, p. 11.
4. Ibid., p. 11.

of urbanism outside the West, Manhattan may have become merely modern due to its relatively modest scale in comparison to global mega cities like Sao Paulo, Kuala Lumpur, Hong Kong, Mexico City or Shanghai; cities which, owing to their mega scale, represent the idea of supermodernity – to borrow a term from Marc Augé. Lest we think that the superficial opposition between the modern and the supermodern renders a true picture and proper account of the thorough deracination of the West against which the non-West triumphs, the modern may stand for the terminal, but the supermodern is belated, untimely; the supreme signifier for the complete banalisation of modern architecture.

This crucial dialectic in terminal modernity illustrated by the rich cycle of obsolescence and rejuvenation exemplifies the ethos of *Manhattanism*. In his retroactive manifesto, Koolhaas offers the view that far from being grounded in some empirical foundationalism, his book 'describes a *theoretical* Manhattan, *Manhattan as conjecture,* of which the present city is the compromised and imperfect realization'.[3] In other words, the city remains to be built: Manhattan *à venir*. But in such striving only such 'episodes of Manhattan's urbanism' that can offer the 'most visible and convincing' model will be of use so as to 'be read against the torrent of negative analyses that emanates from Manhattan about Manhattan and that has firmly established Manhattan as the *Capital of Perpetual Crisis*. Only through the speculative reconstruction of a perfect Manhattan can its monumental successes and failures be read.'[4]

Manhattanism, therefore, is the anamorphic manifestation of limit and return in modernity. This manifestation, evidenced in the compact between the cycle of obsolescence and rebirth echoes Freud's notion of ceaseless return in the famous *fort/da* scene in *Beyond the Pleasure Principle;* an idea which he developed while observing a child playing with a wooden reel toy with a string attachment. In the game the child would toss this toy over his cot with an exclamation: 'o-o-o', (which Freud

translates as the German word *fort,* meaning 'gone') he then retrieves
the toy heralding its reappearance, as if by magic, with another exclamation (*da,* meaning 'there'). Freud concludes that this was the complete game: disappearance and return, which he inscribed as the human
being's compulsion to repeatedly perform his disappearance and reappearance.[5]

Modernity as such is bound up in this compulsion of repetition. And
nothing embodies it more than the modern city, the apotheosis of which
is Manhattan. Manhattan's game of modernity is its delirium. Manhattan
is delirious in its continuous vertical embodiment of eros and ego.
However, this delirium represents the limit of what a city can be. The
twinning of the phantasmic and destructive as archetypes of the death
drive activates a type of synoptic and polemical writing by Koolhaas that
has grown increasingly apocalyptic in urgency wherein all forms of subjectivity and living arrangements inevitably anticipate their own decline
and return. Does such prognostication make Koolhaas a moralist or an
oracle? Is Koolhaas the new apostle of hope or a critical cynic who knows
that all of modern architecture's putative radicality (including his own)
is *a priori* fated for accelerated entropy and inertia? It takes very little to
identify what this symptom is: progress. And Koolhaas both embraces
and attacks it.

In the city, the skyscraper represents the iconic form of this progress.
But the skyscraper's progress (a combination of engineering ingenuity,
spatial compression and repetition in a *gesamtkunstwerk* of linked func-
tions), like the rake's progress consistently faces its own limit and decline.
Especially since the events of 9/11, the skyscraper no longer defines the
phallic gesture of Western superiority and progress over other cultures.
With the repetitive, looped image of the two crumbling towers of the
World Trade Center in lower Manhattan, we are forced to face the decline

of the skyscraper, as it lapses back to the iron age of terminal modernity. In other words the skyscraper is today obsolete not because of its lack of functionality and efficiency, but rather, as a modern emblem of progress it has entered into a stage of uncertainty. Like many forms of modern utopia, the upward thrust of the skyscraper no longer calls forth emancipatory ideals, rather today it may in fact appear not only conservative but also reactionary. Which begs the question: what form of architecture will replace its spatial efficiency?

In a canny transition from the unabashed celebration of the 'culture of congestion' to what he deplores now as 'junkspace' (those excess spaces of arbitrary building schemes which only reproduce non-spaces[6] much like Robert Smithson's identification of the remainders of the industrial wasteland as non-sites of modernity), Koolhaas's treatment of the city as tabula rasa reminds us that one way of understanding cities is not through the methodological application of the theories often found in the discipline of urbanism alone, but also by the coupling of the anthropological and the ethnographic. Smithson for instance treated his non-sites like an archaeological site for his artistic venture. Gordon Matta-Clark worked much the same way but through an inverse logic of poetic violence, embracing the anarchic in order to destructure the excessive spaces of urban blight.

The treatment of the city tissue as part of the remains of modernity harks closely to the work done by Smithson and Clark, but is also connected to the critical scheme of the Situationist International's attack on the city. As Koolhaas famously stated in the opening lines of *Delirious New York,* Manhattan and its multiplicity of phantom forms is 'a moun-

---

5. Sigmund Freud, 'Beyond the Pleasure Principle', in: Peter Gay (ed.), *The Freud Reader,* New York 1989.
6. For two perspicacious discussions of the concept of non-space see Michel de Certeau, *The Practice of Everyday Life,* Berkeley 1984 and Marc Augé, *Non-Places: Introduction to an Anthropology of Supermodernity,* translated by John Howe, London/New York 1995.

tain range of evidence without manifesto'. Conversely, he observed that
the inherent weakness of all manifestos is their lack of evidence. These
statements delineate quite clearly Koolhaas's sociological method across
all his projects, namely the idea that the entire history of modernity is
one immense 'mountain range of evidence' to be investigated and
analysed through a kind of painstaking anthropology; from which whole
manifestos and speculative theories could be written. Observing the work
precipitated so far in his *Project on the City* research such as *Shopping,*
The Great Leap Forward: Pearl River Delta, Lagos, and the exhibition
Mutations, it is possible to glean from the data supplied by these endeav-
ors the extent to which Koolhaas's methodology has been fascinated with
both the exorbitant values of modernity and modernisation (the Asian
cacophony and technophilia), as well as its nightmare scenario (Lagos'
radiological urbanscape). The painstaking combing of the mountain
range is therefore extractive, mobilising theoretical models, new narratives, texts, representations by linking temporalities (past and future);
spatialities (near and faraway, elsewhere and nowhere, sites and non-
sites); and conditions (Utopia and dystopia). As such, urban and social
phenomena often associated with modernity have been grist for the mill
of Koolhaasian meditation and manifesto writing.

In the discourse of the techno-scientific culture of new information
processing systems that drive globalisation everything is either linked or
networked. Capital, culture, cities, desires, catastrophes, etcetera make
up this compost: a reordering and othering of relationships, be it 9/11
or the Iraqi war, the Asian economic meltdown or the Argentinean
implosion, the environmental disaster on the coast of Spain or the
refugee crisis in Australia, nothing escapes the panoptic reach of the new
information system that oversees the emergent simultaneity of global
cause and effect. Globalisation is thus both distortive and affective in its
procedures of organising and arranging vision. The central idea that

seeks to grasp this phenomenological reshaping of consciousness is predicated less on a hierarchy of vertical arrangements of the old imperial
system of colonial domination than on a democratic, open, non-hierar-
chical formation of horizontal arrangements between disparate spaces.
This model of horizontality is at the heart of Koolhaas's new research
on cities. The distinguishing feature of this horizontality is its measure
and flexibility. That is to say, each case-study retains its own specificity
within a general phenomenological system of differentiations. Therefore
the affective logic of each spatial analysis is predicated on its variability.

Master Builder as Epithet

There is a familiar and enduring epithet throughout history for architects, at once heroic and hyperbolic: master builder. The twentieth century has done more to cement and expand this popular image to the
degree that modern architects (Le Corbusier, Mies van der Rohe, Frank
Lloyd Wright, and today Frank Ghery) occupy as much space in the cultural imaginary as artists in the pantheon of great masters. More recently, the architect as master builder and supreme form giver is no longer
just a heroic figure, and, he and his buildings have become creatures of
popular myth and deification, symbols and icons of progress. However,
the postmodern architect increasingly enjoys a less exalted status than
his modernist precursor. As such, the postmodern architect is an ambiva-
lent figure. Neither god nor myth, he exists somewhere in between:
between the spectacle culture of late twentieth century capitalism and
the onerous demands of globalisation that have further deracinated the
heterogeneity of contemporary culture. In this, according to Koolhaas,
modern architecture is a culprit and the postmodern architect the chief
conspirator. Architecture has become obsolete, brought low by the proliferation of junkspace: that which 'remains after modernization has run
its course, or, more precisely, what coagulates while modernization is in

progress. [And if] Modernization had a rational program: to share the blessings of science, universally ... Junkspace is its apotheosis, or melt-down ...'[7] Junkspace, as the surplus manufacture of useless space or dead space, is least like what architecture was. Therefore it delineates the beginning of the end of architecture and, with it, the death of the archi-tect. The Death of God. Death of the Author. The End of History. We have been down this road before, with the infinite number of 'ends of something', which the postmodern acolytes of Nietzsche bestowed as benediction for their disavowal of canonical knowledge.

While 'Junkspace' is a great diatribe against the architect and archi-tecture, close reading shows that it is a cry by a disconsolate lover. In this regard, Koolhaas is both fervent believer and apostate. He believes in the cultural force of architecture, yet he derides architecture as dead: it mere-ly reproduces junkspace, not architecture as such. Perhaps no other architect fits this mould of cultivated dissidency better than he does. He has so intentionally profaned the idea of the architect as master builder; he has taken simultaneously the position of architect and anti-architect; he has excelled as a designer of complex, formal and poetic architectur-al structures and structures that are risibly anti-architecture (one thinks of the makeshift pavilions of Thomas Hirschhorn's monuments and kiosks). More than any architect working today, Koolhaas enjoys the enviable capacity of being able to generate wild admiration and oppro-brium at the same time. In a recent conference[8] in Lagos, Nigeria, the full room was evenly divided between opposing camps of supporters (mostly enthusiastic young students) and detractors (older observers, less sanguine about his theory of Lagos).

7. See Rem Koolhaas, 'Junkspace', *October* No. 100, Spring, 2002, p. 175.
8. Koolhaas was one of the principal speakers at the conference *Under Siege: Four African Cities, Freetown, Johannesburg, Kinshasa, Lagos* organised in March, 2002 by Documenta 11 in Lagos, Nigeria.

This is much the same across the globe: in Asia, Europe, South America and the United States. In a nutshell, he has a simple message: change is good, and we, like the architect, can be agents of change, especially in a global terrain undergoing unprecedented structural, economical, political, social, technological, and cultural transformations. Therefore for architecture to be successful, it must embed itself in the living tissue and social fabric of this new cultural turn. The architect must not become the hermeneutic savant of space, but operate in it like a virus, between forms, social conditions, economic structures, political ideologies. In other words the core of Koolhaas's praxis of architecture and urbanism is exemplified by what could be called the subjectivity of living space. A space that is not simply contingent, but one that functions like a horizontal laboratory of experimentation and co-habitation between disciplinary and institutional formations, communities, desires, and refusals. This horizontal laboratory system has been recently borrowed successfully by a number of innovative exhibitions of art such as *Cities on the Move; Laboratorium,* and most recently *Utopia Station* at the recent Venice Biennale, which have in turn spawned smaller projects such as the work of Hamburg-based Park Fiction group; Milano-based Multiplicity, and Genova-based A12 among others in the artistic sphere who find his message inspiring.

What lessons does he bring back to the great Western metropolis? The idea of horizontality prevalent in the work arrangement of his practice is thus best seen in the simultaneity of Koolhaas's and his eponymous architectural studio's: Office of Metropolitan Architecture (OMA's) involuted involvement in several projects across the terrain of culture and architecture. A typical viral attack on the traditional institutions of modernity is his proposal for the Museum of Modern Art expansion in New York. Here is how Koolhaas and his team thought of the museum and the urban carpet:

The city should be admitted to the Museum. The ground floor is reconsidered as a single urban surface. The sculpture garden is lowered, so that its perimeter can inject daylight into the former basement. Because the sculpture garden is sunken, the wall that now surrounds it disappears. This creates a direct visual transparency between 53rd and 54th streets. The two streets acquire a potential equivalence that allows a large variety of entry and exit points and the orchestration of the different flows of visitors. The new level of the sculpture garden is extended as a garden/moat around the entire perimeter of the ground floor, which becomes in its entirety a metropolitan island.[9]

The Multiple Conditions of Modernity: The Architect as Ethnographer
Yet, if we must, let us imagine together the architect of modernity – despite his incommensurable task – as one who does more than build fantastic, glittering structures; but as the thinking, critical surveyor of the totality of the built, the unbuilt and yet to be built, in the procession of which are refracted the changing conditions of the modern: from modernity to postmodernity to supermodernity.[10] In this sense modernity is not singular: it is a condition of change adapted to each cultural and historical context. *Pace* Koolhaas, let us also observe the architect of modernity as an ethnographer doing fieldwork in the beyond of the Western urban system as he drives his stakes into the involuted urban skein of the second and third worlds. Let's think of him as an anthropologist of terminal modernity scratching beneath the top soil of ruined cities to get to the sickness of what passes for urbanism today. By cross-

9. Architect's statement , Museum of Modern Art, New York in 'Building the New MoMA', in www.moma.org.
10. I borrow this term from Marc Augé in his exemplary book Non-Places: Introduction to an Anthropology of Supermodernity, London/New York 1995. I shall be using this term not just in the sense of a superior kind of modernity, but as a form of critical interruption in the dialectical program that has animated most of the discourse between modernity and postmodernity.
11. Rem Koolhaas, 'Lagos' in: Rem Koolhaas, Stefano Boeri, et. al., *Mutations,* Bordeaux / Barcelona 2000, p. 652.

ing the disciplines of ethnography and anthropology we may perhaps notice the remarkable paradigm shift that drives Koolhaas's recent *Project on the City,* first elaborated in the *Pearl River Delta* research, then in *Shopping,* and recently in *Lagos.* However, this paradigm shift is best understood in tactical and strategic terms, as ways for Koolhaas to enter smoothly into the heart of otherness, that is to say into the space of non-Western modernity. When I use the terms ethnographer and anthropologist I use them as positive terms; as disciplinary tools deployed at the service of understanding human habitat and culture.

Yet, one must ask, what exactly does Koolhaas bring to non-Western modernity beyond the tarnished afterglow of Western rationality? What exactly are his investments in Asia and Africa beyond the expansion of Koolhaasian conglomeratisation of architecture and urbanism? Are the non-Western cities that preoccupy him today truly incubators of the future prospect of the global city as he has ceaselessly promoted them, or are they foils for a different order of theoretical totalisation that many uneasily label neo-colonial? And why must one embrace the idea of endless mutations as the positive logical outcome for cities such as Lagos, in which the architect rides on the poetics of decay and the disorganised arrangement of the third world city as salutary forms of self-organisation? As he writes in the catalogue of the exhibition Mutations, which he organised:

> Lagos, as an icon of West African urbanity, inverts every essential characteristic of the so-called modern city. Yet, it is still – for lack of better word – a city; and one that works.
> Anguish over its shortcomings in traditional urban systems obscures the reasons for the continued, exuberant existence of Lagos and other megacities like it. These shortcomings have generated ingenious, critical alternative systems, which demand a redefinition of ideas such as carrying capacity, stability, and even order.[11]

On the face of it, this observation makes perfect sense, but only if we
were not observing a truly dysfunctional scenario: a city that has completely come unmoored from its previous rational urban logic. Based on
the unambiguous data on the ground, it may be important to inquire as
to what Koolhaas and his research were exactly looking at. For it seems
that the research has not only glossed some of the data but has also been
aperceptive in its idealisation of Lagos' desperation, its implosion into a
tertiary state of pre-urbanity. The fantastic blend of the erotic and the
quotidian in a place like Lagos brings into such a serious study in experimental urbanism the quality of an anthropology of the elsewhere,
whether intentional or not. It is here that one must confront what Marc
Augé called 'the ethnologist's capacity for generalization'.[12] This capacity
for generalisation awards the global architect turned ethnologist not just
an undue advantage, it invests him with an aura of power, inoculates
him against local resistance to his anthropo-urbanism. For, if the exotic
in the global domain cannot be redeemed, it must be either converted
or incorporated into its project.

A critic of Koolhaas's capacity for generalisation has baptised his
recent efforts at the anthropology of the elsewhere as 'drive-by urbanism'. While such criticism may ultimately be unfair, the scepticism of
critics like him perhaps pays off in this scenario sketched in the conclud-
ing remarks of Koolhaas's prologue on Lagos:

> We are resisting the notion that Lagos represents an African city en
> route to becoming modern in a valid, 'African' way. Rather, we think
> it possible to argue that Lagos represents a developed, extreme para-
> digmatic case-study of a city at the forefront of globalizing moderni-
> ty. This is to say that Lagos is not catching up with us. Rather, we may
> be catching up with Lagos. The African city forces the reconceptual-
> ization of the city itself. The fact that many of the trends of modern,
> Western cities can be seen in hyperbolic guise in Lagos suggests that

to write about the African city is to write about the terminal condition of Chicago, London, or Los Angeles.[13]

With such opposition between West and non-West, European order and African disorder, modernity and its other, the elephantiasis of Lagos' urbanism as a warning, is nothing short of a nightmare scenario that urges Western cities to clean up their act. Perhaps it is the case made in behalf of modernity and the idea of the modern that deserves attention. For this reason, I return once more to the outline with which I began: Koolhaas's meditation on Western modernity, on the dialectic of obsolescence and renewal prevalent in Western architecture.

As I mentioned, at the inception of his work, Koolhaas was much concerned with the varied conditions of the modern or modernity as a changing cycle of events that continuously fuses the past and future. Part of the appeal of his work is his ability to think of his projects in historical terms. By thinking of culture, of architecture and urban design historically, he places them not only within the context of transformations in the reception of modernity, but also in the context of interventions within modernity. What his work has shown across the spectrum in which it is engaged, is not necessarily to link cause and effect, that is to say to connect the dots; it is to take a speculative idea and make immanent large theories through the superior ability and capacity for calculation and canniness; and thereby to totalise and organise in one comprehensive, systematic fashion a theory of everything. Paradoxically, it is this very propensity to totalise that is partly the strength of his work involving non-Western urban ecologies. However, this does not mean there are no weaknesses to this approach. For instance, the research project on Lagos could be more properly localised – sometimes the research

12. Marc Augé, op. cit., p. 14.
13. Rem Koolhaas, op. cit., p. 653.

is not historically embedded enough to take advantage of the rich complexity which Lagos offers. Which unfortunately can lead to either unnecessary reductions, unseemly aggrandisement of highly stressful situations in the lives of ordinary citizens in Lagos, and the celebration of the pathological; the glorification of informality, the unstable and the culture of make-do. There is a sense that the attentiveness to these conditions in Lagos tend to focus less on a principle of empathy and more on the erotics of chaos and gigantic flux.

But in spite of the functionalist separation between Lagos and 'better' organised modern cities, cities are not inert data waiting to be dug up and analysed like archaeological ruins, they are living organisms of complex cellular and molecular composition. The African and Asian cities more so, especially when imbricated by the knowledge that their numinous spaces are caught within the contesting discourses of colonialism and post-colonialism; tradition and modernity. With anthropo-urbanism in the mix, we may add neo-colonialism. As Achille Mbembe has argued, though 'the postcolony is chaotically pluralistic; it has nonetheless, an internal coherence'.[14] And for the anthropologist and ethnographer this calls for a review of his method. In this case Koolhaas's work in Asia, offers another vantage point to engage his work. Asia is the Petri dish where one could observe simultaneously the formal intuitions of the 'culture of congestion' along with its expansion due to the unprecedented level of modernisation and urban development occurring there. It is in the context of this development, of the city in the making, that he could truly observe how cities are formed. So, in Asia, the idea of junkspace as non-architecture is revised, it is the architecture: the future has

14. Achille Mbembe, *On the Postcolony*, Berkeley 2001, p. 102.
15. Marc Augé, op. cit., p. 13.
16. Jean-Louis Cohen, 'The Rational Rebel, or the Urban Agenda of OMA' in: Jacques Lucan (ed.), *OMA/Rem Koolhaas*, New York 1991, p. 9.

arrived. But let us return to the question of method in relation to an anthropology of elsewhere; of non-Western modernity. According to Augé:

> The aspect of method, the need for effective contact with interlocutors, is one thing. The representativeness of the chosen group is another: in effect, it is a matter of being able to assess what the people we see and speak to tell us about the people we do not see and speak to. The field ethnologist's activity throughout is the activity of a social surveyor, a manipulator of scales, a low-level comparative language expert: he cobbles together a significant universe by exploring intermediate universes at need, in rapid surveys; or by consulting relevant documents as a historian.[15]

Despite the attempt by the architect to speak authoritatively about the site of his anthropology, it is nevertheless obvious that he may never fully nor properly possess the code that can allow his language to be transformed enough so as to master the elsewhere. This is the challenge of the urban site as a field of ethnographic and anthropological inquiry. Lagos and Asia prove this point well, in the way that they resist Koolhaas's complete mastery.

Conclusion: Theory and Praxis Relinked

Hailed as a visionary by those who believe in the seductive power of his innovative thinking as an architect/theorist and as perverse by those who view him as a tireless self-promoter, Koolhaas has put paid to the idea of the architect as master builder (and the reasons why become more and more clear in his provocations), but also he has reinvented the architect as a different kind of actor/agent in the global terrain. More than a decade ago, just as his work began to enjoy broad recognition and interest, a typical essay began like this: 'Serene provocator, silent dynamiter, Rem Koolhaas has worked for fifteen years as an extraordinary commentator on the condition of late twentieth century.'[16]

Analysis of Koolhaas's work was awash with this type of praise. As already noted above, Koolhaas's work remains the flashpoint of much controversy. And today as his buildings begin to be realised, as his global ambitions expand and his treatment of the entire global cultural landscape as fodder for theories of interventionist urbanism – Lagos, Pearl River Delta, Shopping, the Schiphol Airport project, Museum of Modern Art, Manhattan, etcetera – proliferates the very identity of his work is also changing. For, Rem Koolhaas©, in a typical global fashion, has become a conglomerate. His ideas no longer stand just for the radicality of architecture's expansive cultural site, including its critique and analysis, they stand for many other interests beyond architecture that presently seem not quite radical but may be dangerously callow in some instances such as the venture with Prada.

Yet no one can deny the fact that Koolhaas's ideas have left a huge impact on our thinking. In spite of his detractors, these ideas have precious little to do with self-promotion and more with his brilliant capacity for synthesis and attraction to all that is difficult like that Himalaya of evidence waiting to be scaled. Therefore, an exhibition of his and OMA's work at the quarter century mark of the office's founding, is indeed a welcome event. The frenetic pace of building projects, research, consultancy, urban speculation, exhibitions, publications, etcetera, calls for a method to encapsulate (if that were possible) what OMA stands for. While the salutary effect of his work is clear, this is not a paean to the contemporary architect as superhero flitting between the arboreal network of concrete and metallic vertical spires that threaten to perforate the soft cap of the sky. Nor is it about the worn cliché of the incandescent supernova outburning all other celestial bodies in the bright distant sky of the future. It is not an ode to the chief pedagogue of modernity and Utopia either, even if architecture often lends itself to exacerbating the changing conditions of the modern.

Koolhaas has recently reconsidered what the office structure of a global architect/theorist should be. The strategic combination of OMA/AMO seems like an attempt to integrate two cultures that for a long time formed independent nuclei in Koolhaas's practice, namely research and building or thinking and doing. While OMA represents the architectural studio, the idea hub of experiments in postmodern architectural forms, AMO is the inverse of OMA, which is the transformation of research into a commodity in the global culture of multinational consultancy. To inseminate research into the market seems again a move produced to exploit the glut of cash available at the till of global capitalism. Koolhaas, like Guy Debord, grasped that the spectacle of capitalism is the rule of neo-liberal modernity rather than the exception. However, unlike Debord's scabrous, critique of capitalism, Koolhaas rather understands the mediation of social life by capitalism as an opportunity to relink the capitalist consumer to his fate. These intersections are characteristic strategic interventions produced to enact a radical effect in relation to art, culture, technology, space, and society. The program for this inexorable drive to define an encompassing territory of research and action was put in place twenty-five years ago, when his seminal study of Manhattan first appeared in *Delirious New York.*[17] However, this book began with a different kind of promise than what it has turned out to be in the complicated transformations that Koolhaas's work has undergone since the book first appeared.

I would like to thank Muna El Fituri-Enwezor for her careful reading of this essay and for her editorial comments throughout its writing.

17. First published in 1978, and reissued in 1994, *Delirious New York,* like the Situationist manifesto in relation to modernism, has become a classic intervention within the urban discourse of postmodernism.

It is Rem Koolhaas's contribution, 'Junkspace', an extraordinary piece of writing that is both a postmodern artefact in its own right, and – a whole new aesthetic perhaps? unless it is a whole new vision of history. . . . But first we have to look at the writing itself, whose combination of revulsion and euphoria is unique to the postmodern in a number of instructive ways. . . .

We are henceforth in the realm of the formless (Rosalind Krauss, out of Bataille); but 'formlessness is still form, the formless also a typology'. It is not quite the 'anything goes' of the new generation of computer-generating 'blob architects' (Greg Lynn, Ben van Berkel): 'in fact, the secret of Junkspace is that it is both promiscuous *and* repressive: as the formless proliferates, the formal withers, and with it all rules, regulations, recourse.' Shades of Marcuse and repressive tolerance? 'Junkspace is a Bermuda triangle of concepts, a petri dish abandoned: it cancels distinctions, undermines resolve, confuses intention with realization. It replaces hierarchy with accumulation, composition with addition. More and more, more is more. Junkspace is overripe and undernourishing at the same time, a colossal security blanket that covers the earth in a stranglehold of care . . . Junkspace is like being condemned to a perpetual Jacuzzi with millions of your best friends . . . A fuzzy empire of blur, it fuses high and low, public and private, straight and bent, bloated and starved to offer a seamless patchwork of the permanently disjointed.'

There are no doubt still 'trajectories' with their magical moments: 'Postmodernism adds a crumple-zone of viral *poché* that fractures and multiplies the endless frontline of display, a peristaltic shrink-wrap crucial to all commercial exchange. Trajectories are launched as ramp, turn horizontal without any warning, intersect, fold down, suddenly emerge on a vertiginous balcony above a large void. Fascism without dictator. From the sudden dead end where you were dropped by a monumental, granite staircase, an escalator takes you to an invisible destination, facing a provisional vista of plaster, inspired by forgettable sources.'

There are also, in this churning pseudo-temporality of matter ceaselessly mutating all around us, moments of rare, of breathtaking beauty: railway stations unfold like iron butterflies, airports glisten like cyclopic dewdrops, bridges span often negligible banks like grotesquely enlarged versions of the harp. To each rivulet its own Calatrava.' But such moments are scarcely enough to compensate for the nightmare, or to make the hallucinations all worthwhile. Cyberpunk seems to be a reference to grasp at here, which – like Koolhaas, only ambiguously cynical – seems positively to revel in its own (and its world's) excess. But cyberpunk is not really apocalyptic, and I think the better coordinate is Ballard, the Ballard of the multiple 'end-of-the-worlds', minus the Byronic melancholy and the rich orchestral pessimism and *Weltschmerz*.

For it is the end of the world that is in question here; and that could be exhilarating if apocalypse were the only way of imagining that world's disappearance (whether we have to do here with the bang or the whimper is not the interesting question). It is the old world that deserves the bile and the satire, this new one is merely its own self-effacement, and its slippage into what Dick called kipple or gubble, what LeGuin once described as the buildings 'melting. They were getting soggy and shaky, like jello left out in the sun. The corners had already run down the sides, leaving great creamy smears.' Someone once said that it is easier to imagine the end of the world than to imagine the end of capitalism. We can now revise that and witness the attempt to imagine capitalism by way of imagining the end of the world.

But I think it would be better to characterize all this in terms of History, a History that we cannot imagine except as ending, and whose future seems to be nothing but a monotonous repetition of what is already here. The problem is then how to locate radical difference; how to jumpstart the sense of history so that it begins again to transmit feeble signals of time, of otherness, of change, of Utopia. The problem to be solved is that of breaking out of the windless present of the postmodern back into real historical time, and a history made by human beings. I think this writing is a way of doing that or at least of trying to. Its science-fictionality derives from the secret method of this genre: which in the absence of a future focuses on a single baleful tendency, one that it expands and expands until the tendency itself becomes apocalyptic and explodes the world in which we are trapped into innumerable shards and atoms. The dystopian appearance is thus only the sharp edge inserted into the seamless Moebius strip of late capitalism, the punctum or perceptual obsession that sees one thread, any thread, through to its predictable end.

Yet this alone is not enough: a breaking of the sound barrier of History is to be achieved in a situation in which the historical imagination is paralysed and cocooned, as though by a predator's sting: no way to burst through into the future, to reconquer difference, let alone Utopia, except by writing yourself into it, but without turning back. It is the writing that is the battering ram, the delirious repetition that hammers away at this sameness running through all the forms of our existence (space, parking, shopping, working, eating, building) and pummels them into admitting their own standardized identity with each other, beyond colour, beyond texture, the formless blandness that is no longer even the plastic, vinyl or rubber of yesteryear. The sentences are the boom of this repetitive insistence, this pounding on the hollowness of space itself; and their energy now foretells the rush and the fresh air, the euphoria of a relief, an orgasmic breaking through into time and history again, into a concrete future.

The Story of K.

Matthew Stadler

Logic is doubtless unshakeable, but it cannot withstand a man who wants to go on living. FRANZ KAFKA, THE TRIAL

The truth of what K. tells us is neither here nor there. He is not a liar; nor is he an oracle. His language is so beautiful it is difficult to imagine K. wordless. What would his architectural practice if it was mute? In his book, *S,M,L,XL* K. stages an example of this impossibility. A model of the proposed City Hall for The Hague is pictured on nine consecutive spreads – no text. The sequence ends in a crescendo of floor plans, the proposed building's twenty-four stories escalating to their pinnacle, a conclusion after which there is nothing. This orchestration is telling. Even without text, K. cannot resist constructing a plot. In the corner of each spread a set of hands is pictured, shifting the parts of the model – the protagonist. On the sixth spread, amidst the protagonist's innocent progress, a woman in a chador holds a wounded child – the subplot. The sequence ends in plans, of which nothing ever came – the tragedy.

As an architect K. is not theory driven so much as he is plot driven. His texts, often brilliant, serve a narrative logic rather than a philosophical one, imbuing architectural choices with meaning by placing them in a story. For example, here is K.'s story of the *Très Grande Bibliothèque*, a very large library for Paris. 'Working with the numbers and the program, we excavated all of the elements that were not public and arrived at a shape that represented the storage. The remaining shape would be represented by the public elements. When we saw this kind of strange being as standing on the banks of the Seine we began to believe we were discovering something. We made a reverse model in which everything that was supposed to be solid was transparent and the voids were solid. Then we invited a series of colleagues and related intellectuals to criticise this approach. Their comments were scathing. They said it would be absolutely awkward, impossible, and ridiculous, but we had to go on at that point. We had no choice.'

K. encounters the derision of his colleagues and must go on. This kind of forced necessity – a negation of will – substitutes for argument or theory repeatedly in the story of K. The negation of will is pursued everywhere: from these narrative accounts of inexorability, through attempts to link design choices to pre-existing, neutral data (as above: 'working with numbers and program' a design is 'arrived at'), to a deliberate blurring of agency within the chaos of the design process. As K. notes repeatedly, 'architecture is a paradoxical drama of simultaneous power and powerlessness'. This is the drama he prefers and that he diagrams in his texts.

'These people are easy to win over', thought K., disturbed only by the silence in the left half of the room, which lay just behind him and from which only one or two isolated handclaps had come.

The antagonists are familiar. Throughout the story of K. hostile and monolithic forces are gathered under the rubric of 'the architectural profession'. Their relation to the protagonist (at once K.'s design firm, OMA, and a quality of being that OMA serves, sometimes called 'the real') gives shape to a prototypical story of heroic return: Modernist ambition and clarity (embodied in predecessors Leonidov, Louis Kahn, or Mies) have been dissolved by the corrosive tendencies of an architectural discourse rooted in linguistics (which K. calls, 'the "de_s"'). In one of his pivotal texts, 'Bigness or the problem of large', K. criticises 'contemporary doctrines that question the possibility of the Whole and the Real as viable categories and resign themselves to architecture's supposedly inevitable disassembly and dissolution'. Against the entropy of these hodgepodge doctrines, K. launches the texts and designs of OMA. The whole and the real are not K.'s objectives so much as they are impossibilities that he is obliged to pursue. It is difficult to sort out any coherent intellectual history behind K.'s use of these terms, particularly 'the real'.

Occurrences of the real are few. It emerges first, in 'Bigness or the problem of large' as an unspecific capacity that is threatened by 'an extended engagement with simulation, virtuality, nonexistence', (a set of tactics by which recent avant gardes have tried to avoid 'the problem of bigness'). Decrying the loss of the real, K. blames 'the generation of May '68', his own, for 'pre-empting architecture's actual disappearance ... [by] experimenting with real or simulated virtuality, reclaiming, in the name of modesty, its former omnipotence in the world of virtual reality (where fascism may be pursued with impunity?)' These minor Fausts, K. implies, have made a poor bargain, winning our eternal expulsion from the real in exchange for dominion over nothing, mere virtuality. K. suggests that architects should refuse this bargain and instead face 'the problem of bigness' by theorising and building big in both the material and the virtual worlds. While K. is painstaking in his description of bigness, he draws the real only in shadow. This central capacity – whose potential loss gives this turn in K.'s story all its urgency – is a void, simply the negative space left by that which has disappeared.

Later uses are scattered. In 'Atlanta', the atrium is described as 'a hermetic interior sealed against the real'. (The real as a truly public space, or unenclosed space?) In 'Whatever Happened to Urbanism?' K. complains that 'according to Baudrillard we cannot be real'. (The real as a condition threatened by philosophy?) In 'Generic City' he argues that 'to the extent that identity is derived from physical substance, from the historical, from context, from the real, we somehow cannot imagine that anything contemporary – made by us – contributes to it'. (The real as the engine of identity and authenticity?) The real is never present, but always under threat. K. positions it as a kind of Eden, an unspecific, lost paradise to which we might return through bigness.

The real can be found in Plato, Berkeley, Hegel, Heidegger, Lacan and countless others. But in all these cases, the philosophical rigor of the discourse burdens the real with a precision and inflexibility that runs at cross-purposes to K.'s. The real, for Lacan or Hegel, must function as a tool that can be picked up and used at other times by other thinkers. As such, it needs a rigidity and clarity that does not interest K. He has no use for this kind of tool, which is called 'theory'. Rather, K. deploys the real as a poetic concept, a kind of viral 'meme', attractive enough to be contagious and malleable enough to survive many contexts and uses. (The best fit, among K.'s antecedents, is with John Dewey and William James, whose pragmatic 'real' affords the same luxurious indeterminacy as the real of K. Yet it is precisely this indeterminacy that weakens the philosophical viability of the pragmatist formulation; in the same way, K.'s 'real' is not philosophical.)

'… It's so horrible here', she said after a pause, taking K.'s hand. 'Do you think you'll manage to improve things?'
'Actually', he said, 'it isn't my place to improve things here, as you put it …'

Adrift from philosophy and architectural theory, K.'s 'real' can find its bearings best in a history largely unknown to him, the work of the late San Francisco poet Jack Spicer. Spicer's project (which similarly circled around a notion of 'the real') aspired to a kind of instrumentality and coherence like what K. pursues, deeply wed to the narrative of his life.

Spicer wrote that 'the real is a composing force that we enact through poetry'. The enactment involved a surrender of the poet's will and tastes to the dictations of an outside voice that Spicer likened, alternately, to radio, Yeats' 'instructors' and also to Martians. While this outside was 'the real', it was not, strictly speaking, 'outside'. Spicer paradoxically insisted that we 'ascend' into the body to contact the real: 'One keeps unmentionable / What one ascends to the real with / The lie / The cock in the other person's mouth / The real defined out of nothing.' Notably, it is not the flesh, exactly, but the hollow space of the body – the nothing of the mouth – that measures and contains the real, so that even as Spicer embeds that idea in flesh he leaves its carnality supremely unresolved. His poems comprise a field of forces that return the ideational into the body without posing either one as the erasure of the other. This, too, is K.'s achievement.

K. is our most profoundly carnal architect, even as he appears to be among our most cerebral. He writes and builds so that theory will fail and our minds fall back into our bodies. K. distrusts systems. His sentences – like the sloping floor of a corridor that draws you toward obstructions or voids – disable the mastery the mind craves (and that coherent theory affords), so that the body (supreme force of the unresolved world) ascends again to power. The real, for K., as for Spicer, is this condition – not a negation of the intellect but the reestablishment of an older, more complex integration that activates patterns of collectivity rooted in the likeness of bodies rather than in ideological imperatives. It naturally frightens or offends those, living, whose bodies are dead. The experience is most vivid at the threshold of a sloping ramp (say, at K.'s Kunsthal in Rotterdam) where the mind is not equipped to navigate the downward pull that leads it toward uncertain terminal points. But precisely this same condition obtains at the threshold of K.'s sentences. For example: 'For urbanists, the belated rediscovery of the virtues of the classical city at the moment of their definitive impossibility may have been the point of no return, fatal moment of disconnection, disqualification. They are now specialists in phantom pain: doctors discussing the intricacies of an amputated limb.'

In the gravity of this utterance we are moved while the mind is robbed of any stable footing so that we fall back into the carnal to find meaning or conviction or certainty. (This vertigo should remind us there is little reason to separate text and building in our observations of K. The two fields of construction operate collusively in his work. There is no differentiation.)

While witnesses to this drama mistake K.'s attacks as the starting place for a new theory, in fact K. has no alternative system to put in place. He does not value theory, but a world in which bodies move outside theory's certainties: 'to understand the city no longer as a tissue, but more as a "mere" coexistence, a series of relationships no longer "caught" in architectural connections.' Released from the imposed coherence of architectural ideas – built or written – individuals are not so much atomised as they are thrown back into themselves. This condition, which K. often praises as 'brutal' or 'bestial', imbues us with radically collective powers and new agency.

How does K. take on this challenge? Here are some of the ways K. describes his operations: 'to concretize speculative systems in the present society as a method of acquiring reality for them, regardless of their truth'; 'to be alert to the delicacies that can exist within the bureaucratic, instrumentalized world'; 'try to find the concept through which the worthless turns into something where even the sublime is not unthinkable'; 'the exploitation of the previously unthinkable'; 'investigate whether the inevitable contains the sublime'; 'combine indeterminacy with architectural specificity'; 'feel simultaneous glee and horror'.

All told, these operations comprise what Spicer called 'a disordered devotion towards the real'. The fragment, from Spicer's notebook of 1964, a year before his death, reads: '… a disordered devotion towards the real / A death note. With fifteen cents and real / Estate I could ride a subway in New York. No / Poet starved. They died of it.' This curious intersection of poetry, vitality, and death is immediately familiar to the student of K. Morbidity pervades the story of K., embedded permanently in the will toward creation. That Spicer locates this intersection in New York provides a pivot away from which these two poets of the real can be seen to diverge. Spicer despised New York, feelings its heat and congestion as a kind of inhuman emanation – whatever is real in New York becomes real estate. K. saw a world of new possibilities in the grid of real estate, not an erasure of the real. Where Spicer foresaw the death of the poet in the clutches of this intoxicating grid, K. remains blind to it.

Could K.'s body possibly be meditating a revolution and preparing a new trial for him, since he was withstanding the old one with such ease?

Spicer made texts to invigorate the real: 'Words are what stick to the real. We use them to push the real, to drag the real into the poem.' K. puts it differently: 'I am unwilling to abandon the role of the writer, simply because it represents other worlds, other life notions, other perspectives.' K. pursues the same ends through buildings and cities (which Spicer called 'a movement of poetry'). The city is for Spicer 'not merely a system of belief but their beliefs and their hearts living together'. This city, composed not of systems but of adjacencies, is the same that K. envisions when he aspires to understand the city 'no longer as a tissue, but more as a "mere" coexistence, a series of relationships'. In both of these projects the ascendancy of the flesh – through words and buildings – invigorates the real by displacing disembodied certainties such as theory and system.

Spicer's reflections on the city and text conclude: 'They are angry at their differences – the dead and the living, the ghosts and the angels, the green parrot and the dog I have just invented. All things that use separate words. They want to inhabit the city.

'But the city in that sense is as far from me (and the things that speak through me) as Dante was from Florence. Farther. For it is a city that I do not remember.

'But the city that we create in our bartalk or in our fuss and fury about each other is in an utterly mixed and mirrored way an image of the city. A return from exile.'

Those who knew Spicer know that he lived most happily, most completely, talking in a bar. On that barstool, in his fuss and fury, talk returned Spicer into his body – a body, at once numbed and excited by alcohol and company so that he could bear to inhabit it. This utterly mixed and mirrored condition, 'an image of the city', was also the real.

What faces these were around him! Their little black eyes darted furtively from side to side, their beards were stiff and brittle, and to take hold of them would be like clutching bunches of claws rather than beards.

'The real' of K. is not only textual but also oratorical. Wed to the body, when K. utters it in speech, 'the real' quickens the listener's pulse. At a public forum concerning the Seattle Public Library, K. was asked how his design would ensure the safety of children. K. stiffened, as he sometimes does, and drew himself up. 'Children', he said, 'are underestimated by adults. They have a frankness and directness, an engagement with the real that gives them more savvy than adults might think.' K. saw no need to protect kids in the library, except in so far we can protect them from condescension. The crowd of 700 people, and especially the panel of fourteen who were choosing the architect, were audibly moved by this bracing sentiment, particularly its monad-like node of central meaning, 'the real'. The story of K. has been shaped by such oral performance, repeated over and over as if for a tribe of illiterates. He has given innumerable public speeches in the last twenty years of his practice. Add to this the countless conferences and client meetings that make up the vast bulk of the architect's duties, and one begins to recognise that professional architecture is largely formed and propagated through a kind of oral transmission. It is, at the very least, what Walter Ong, in his book, *Orality and Literacy,* calls 'a culture with a still massive oral residue'.

What kind of discourse does orality shape? Ong says that an oral tradition is aggregative rather than analytical; additive rather than subordinative; situational rather than abstract; it is redundant, agnostically toned, homeostatic, participatory, and tends to be conservative. In the case of K. we see evidence of many of these pressures and flat contradictions of others. For example, such novel terminologies as 'the generic city', 'the culture of congestion', or 'junk space' take their place in an additive series of McLuhanesque 'probes' – essentially poetic phrases that are 'merely' launched, piling one on top of the other, rather than being placed in any kind of hierarchical arrangement (say causes and effects, or general conditions and their subordinative manifestations). So, one enters a disordered world of generic congestions and spaces of junk interpenetrating without any kind of instrumental relation.

On the other hand, K. seems predisposed against the situational, having blurred a global cornucopia of situations into such broad abstractions as 'generic city' and 'junk space'. But these abstractions are peculiar. Each is not the distilled essence of a group of particulars, so much as it is the profile formed by a great mound of them. A small part of K.'s description of 'junkspace' illustrates: 'The ceiling is a crumpled plate, like the Alps; grids of unstable tiles alternate with monogrammed sheets of black plastic, improbably punctured by grids of crystal chandeliers … Metal ducts are replaced by breathing textiles. Gaping joints recall vast ceiling voids (former canyons of asbestos?), beams, ducting, rope, cable, insulation, fireproofing, string …' This formulation is not abstract so much as it is hyper-concrete, a totality of situations rather than the superseding of the situational.

K.'s discourse is certainly redundant, agnostically toned (by which Ong means its narrative is rooted in physical conflicts and pressures) and supremely homeostatic, operating entirely on its own terms, its own patterns and logic; it is not, in Ong's sense, participatory (that is, the listener is rarely positioned in 'a close empathetic, communal identification with the known'). Paradoxically, K.'s discourse is profoundly conservative. His abnegation – his dislike of his own will – ensnares him in a drama that ultimately must preserve conditions as they are. Restricting his interventions to 'running the numbers and the program', K. will always 'arrive at' shapes that re-enact – even as they refine and amplify – the conditions that precede his operations. If he is a reformer, he must believe that such intensifications are, like the quickening of a fever, necessary steps toward change. But given the reach and intractability of the conditions he addresses (really, the project of built civilisation), his position is an almost apocalyptic one. Certainly it is one that invites severities that will damage and destroy a great deal on the way toward whatever lies ahead. Further, because K. has no interest in constructing philosophical ideas, his discourse cannot be applied the way theory is applied. Instead, it forms a spectacle that might or might not catalyse other transformational actions.

K. walked rigidly between … The three of them were interlocked in a unity that would have brought all three of them down together had one of them been knocked over. It was a unity such as can hardly be formed except by lifeless matter.

A hopeful closing note in his essay on bigness prefigures the dominant tragedy in the story of K., and its greatest irony: 'Bigness is impersonal: the architect is no longer condemned to stardom.' One should not doubt that this flawed prediction is among the most sincere wishes K. has ever betrayed in his texts, yet its realisation has remained stunningly outside his grasp. K. is trapped as a character in his own narrative; he is the Hero. Ironically, the very nature of his discourse traps him there. Because he abjures systems, K. trades in meanings that depend on the teller and his imagined biography. Adrift from philosophy, these meanings hang on the spine of a life. When K. writes, 'We were building castles in the sand; now we swim in the ocean that washed them away', his poetry conjures meanings that inevitably lead us to imagine personal costs, a long dissolution, the figure of K.

Spicer knew the author would always be sacrificed to this kind of discourse. He saw that a life could not survive it, but must always be used up as material in such projects. 'The poetry / Of the absurd comes through San Francisco / television. Directly connected / with moon rockets. / If this is dictation, it is driving / Me wild.' His own disappearance was rapid, awful, and complete (Spicer's dying words, to his friend Robin Blaser, were 'My vocabulary did this to me. Your love will let you go on'). K.'s drama is played out on stage: the private man erased by the spectacle of his discourse. As his discourse casts its spell, K. comes into our view – caught between the audience and the poetry – trapped in a body that, because it has become conflated with his meanings, stands exposed as both the conduit to and the only obstacle between the maddened crowd and the narrative they desire. Condemned to this stardom by the script he writes, K. cannot find a proper way out.

K. had hoped bigness would mark a change in his fortunes. As he wrote it, 'Bigness' invited us to enter a new set of relations, an almost biotic system of interdependencies within which no one element could ever 'star', nor be autonomous, nor even, in a way, be capable of will. He described and beckoned a world without external system, authority, or the possibility of control, and yet he did so wearing the medals of an authority he despised – the hero. So long as he speaks and writes as he does – using a poetic narrative to give meaning and force to his utterance – K. will remain in this trap of his own making, his body an oracle against his wishes.

K. now perceived clearly that he was supposed to seize the knife himself, as it traveled from hand to hand above him, and plunge it into his own breast.

About half-way through S,M,L,XL, K. recalls a dream:

I was walking with Jan Voorberg, my partner at the time. He was an architect from The Hague, exactly my age, but small and blond.

We were walking together along the edge of a river on a kind of sinking boardwalk.

That typified our situation – every moment of the week, our position was slowly sinking in the general swamp, and we constantly had to try to uplift and inspire each other.

So, half sinking, I said, 'Well, in a way it's interesting to walk along a river on a sinking boardwalk – don't you think?'

We were both wearing shorts and were wet to our waists.

'Yes,' he said. 'It is interesting … but it's completely different from taking a dry walk.'

When we got to the end of the river, there was an enormous abyss.

Hesitantly, we both looked over the edge.

'Well, it's not that deep,' I said.

'No,' he said, 'it's not. And the wall isn't all that steep. I think if we're really careful, we can almost walk down. Yeah, we may have to walk kind of diagonally, but I think we can do it.'

So, encouraging each other, we started our descent. And of course, before we knew it, we were falling. Tumbling down this cliff, I could see that we were going to crash over a small meadow, where, on a tiny piece of green grass, there was an enormous group of people having a picnic. I knew right away it was a picnic – there was a large white sheet and the entire group was sitting around it.

So, still falling, I thought, 'How should I land? How can I maneuver to avoid the people? How can I crash without making a desperate mess of this picnic?' I worked out a trajectory in my mind. I thought it would work amazingly.

I hit the ground and made a few leaps, successfully avoiding everybody. But then, at the very last moment, there was a sick, soft feeling in my heel.

'My God, Jan, I hit it!' I hardly dared to touch it. When I felt my heel, there was a bloody mush on my fingers. Then I turned around and saw a small gap in the ground, with a baby whose head I had smashed.

It would be over-reaching to suggest that this one, perfect dream forms a template for K.'s practice and his texts. Yet this, more or less, is the story of K.

Thank to Richard Jensen for conversations that helped form this essay and for the suggestion to include Jack Spicer.

136   RENÉ BOOMKENS, EEN DREMPELWERELD, MODERNE ERVARING EN STEDELIJKE OPENBAARHEID,

ROTTERDAM, 1998, PP. 367-368

With his emphasis on an architecture that represents the unconscious and on the 'practice of panic' that characterizes late-modern city existence, Koolhaas comes quite close to formulations chosen by Walter Benjamin to describe the modern urban experience. Koolhaas's imagery is expressly inspired by the same Baudelairean worldview that defined Benjamin's vision of the big city. Shocks, coincidence, moment, ephemera, unconscious: the 'generic city' does not differ in principle, at any rate, from the city of flaneurs – at most modernization and urbanization are progressing at a faster pace. And there is a great deal of evidence that Koolhaas intends ... to engage this urban 'panic' with equal means: parry the shocks with new shocks. Koolhaas's scenario for the 'generic city', his urban-planning choice for 'bigness' and his thorough loathing for anything that smells of history, his explicit choice against any architectural style and for speed, superficiality and the eclecticism of postmodernism together form a curious melding of the late-Romantic modernism of Baudelaire and the tabula rasa of the avant-gardes. From the former, Koolhaas adopted the empathy with the frenetic culture of the city, but not the tragic awareness of loss or the melancholy. From the latter, he took up the love of destruction, the breaking of ground and the creation of space, but he rejected any idea or ideal of planning, and certainly any reference to spatial equilibrium, to the radical separation of functions or to the social or even moral significance of architecture or urban planning. Furthermore he seems to have traded the concept of a one-off tabula rasa for one of a continually self-repeating practive of interaction of existing situations, and he has opted for a sort of ad hoc city as a hectic enclave in an otherwise empty, or rather overgrown environment... Quite consciously Koolhaas has driven us to the limits of any urban experience, and leaves us, as a good post-modernist – or better yet, deconstructivist – in the dark as to his own assessment of the 'generic city' as the standard city of the coming century.

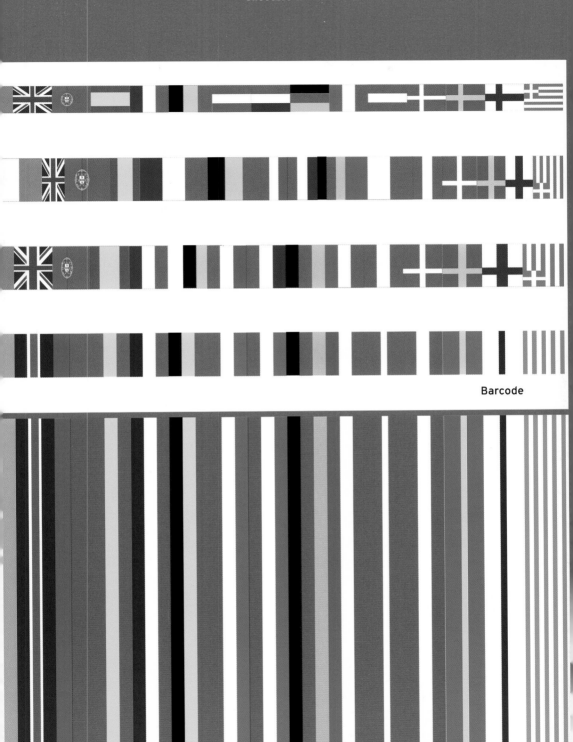

Barcode

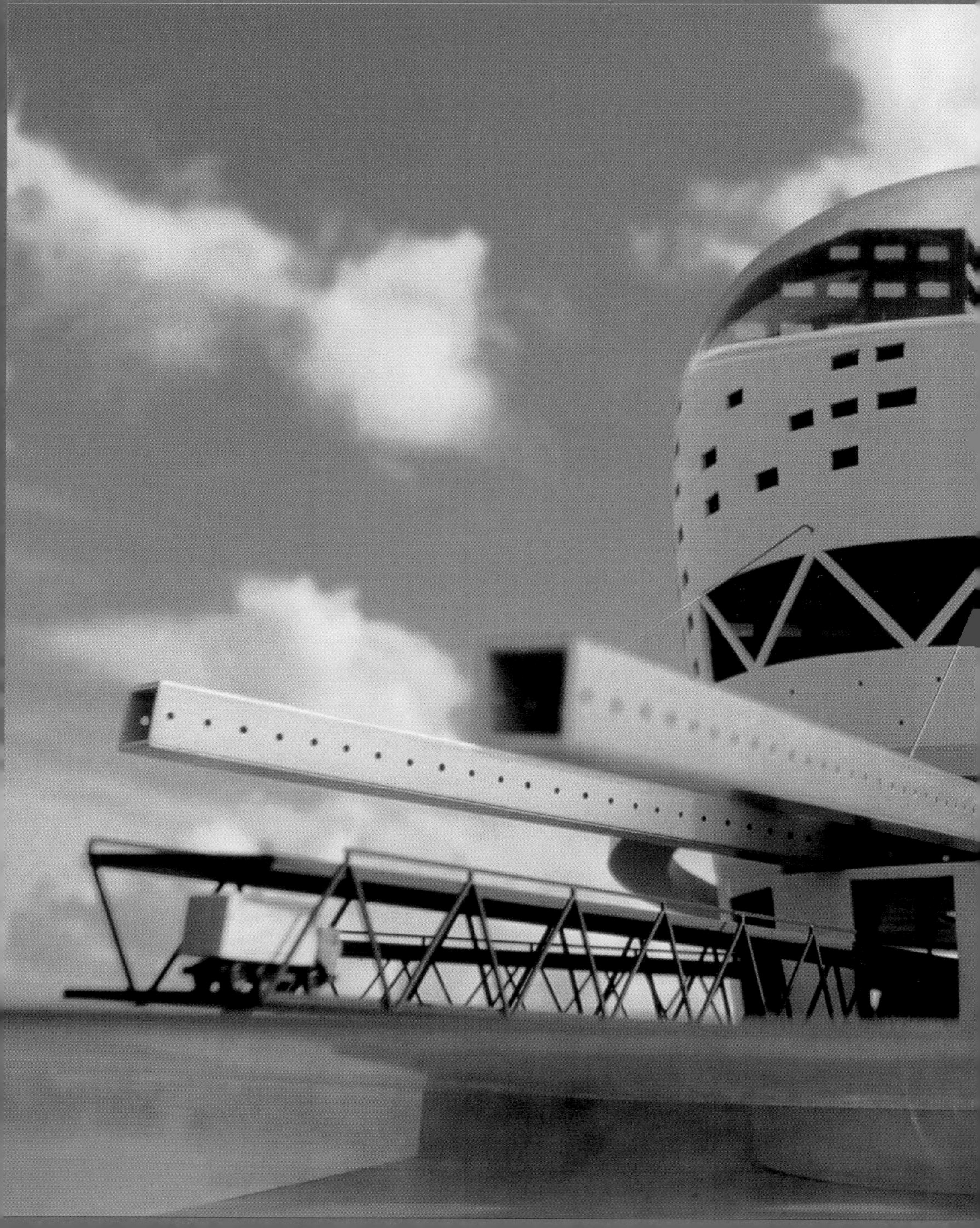

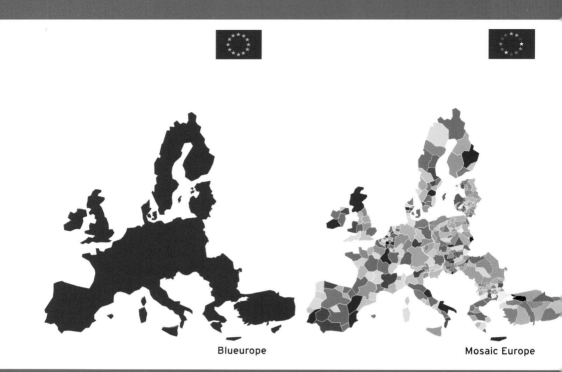

Blueurope

Mosaic Europe

Religious Diversity

Political Diversity

€urope

Cool Europe

AREA

Bart Verschaffel
Fritz Neumeyer
Bruce Sterling
Sarah Whiting

The Survival Ethics of Rem Koolhaas: The First Houses by OMA

Bart Verschaffel

And just as it happens that in a great crush of humanity, when the people push against each other, no one can fall down without drawing along another, and those that are in front cause destruction to those behind – this same thing you may see happening everywhere in life. No man can go wrong to his own hurt only, but he will be both the cause and the sponsor of another's wrongdoing. For it is dangerous to attach one's self to the crowd in front, and so long as each one of us is more willing to trust another than to judge for himself, we never show any judgement in the matter of living, but always a blind trust, and a mistake that has been passed on from hand to hand finally involves us and works our destruction. It is the example of other people that is our undoing; let us merely separate ourselves from the crowd, and we shall be made whole.

SENECA, DE VITA BEATA (ON THE GOOD LIFE)[1]

On one of the first pages of *S,M,L,XL* there is a diagram with a long list of OMA employees and the projects that the bureau has worked on.

There are thin lines connecting each project to the finely printed names of the designers or employees who were involved in them. From Rem Koolhaas, who stands at the top of the list of names, there are little lines leading to every single project. Only one thin line, almost imperceptible, leads to the last project: to *Project X*. Hubert Damisch was correct to have written that Koolhaas establishes 'a rare link between a theory and a project'.

Koolhaas formulates his theory in texts and statements. But what exactly is *Project X?* I suppose that *X* is 'everything', in other words, things that Koolhaas himself is busy with – *alone.* OMA seems like a collective enterprise that applies an open design strategy: Koolhaas works with flexible varying and heterogeneous design teams, he combines highly diverse commissions and works in many different parts of the world, he always starts from the given circumstances, and his theoretical discourse is presented in an environment of transformed quotes and images. The work is always about 'outside' and it is full of 'others'. It seems as if Koolhaas never works alone. This optical illusion is the effect of a vanishing trick, the intention of which Koolhaas himself explained in a speech he gave on receiving the Rotterdam-Maaskant Prize in 1986. At the start of that speech he said, 'It is a remarkable feeling, but I am not an I. Throughout my entire career I have only written the word "I" once, and that was in the sentence "I am a ghostwriter". A ghostwriter is someone who does not appear on stage himself, but remains in the background and speaks in the name of someone else.' This statement is unexpected and perhaps even sounds suspect from someone who has grown into one of the most famous and mediagenic architecture stars. Yet in that same 1986 speech, he heralded this 'stardom' as 'a strategy': 'The mythology of the architect begs a reconstruction plan.' Architecture, according to Koolhaas in 1986, can only survive when the architect once again performs as a visionary: publicly, indiscreetly, self-assuredly and with imagination. And this imagination draws its strength from the forgotten potentialities that the ghostwriter, Koolhaas, whispers into the ear of architecture: mass and the large-scale, the tasteless and the formless. At the end of his lecture, however, Koolhaas said, '… intentions such as these can perhaps only be actualized if they are not talked about too explicitly. For this reason, I solemnly request that you, the public, forget what I have just said. From now on, I will keep it to myself.'[2] That, I assume, is the reason for *Project X*.

The introduction to *S,M,L,XL* states that architecture is 'a chaotic adventure' and that the book has no pretences to be coherent. The texts by Koolhaas do not link projects together, but function as independent building blocks; the book 'does not avoid contradiction', and it 'can be read in any way'. This all sounds commendable and reassuring, and many readers can certainly turn this freedom to their advantage, but the guideline does sounds pretty unbelievable. Few books tell readers so explicitly what they must do and what not to expect on the opening pages, and the more circumspect readers will sense that flattering temptations of this sort are sending them up the garden path. Freewheeling might be highly productive, but it is not especially critical, and it conceals the fact that *S,M,L,XL* is an unusually painstakingly composed tome.

Almost twenty years after the Maaskant Prize, now that Koolhaas and OMA have a built *œuvre* that can be tested, we can ascertain how Koolhaas himself has applied 'the forgotten potentialities of architecture' – and not just in theory. Koolhaas later synthesised 'mass' and the 'large-scale' in the key concept 'Bigness'. Mass and scale are both terms that indicate a relationship to an isolated human body which, in proportion

1. Lucius Annasus Seneca, *Moral Essays,* translated by John W. Basore, vol. II, The Loeb Classical Library, London 1928-1935.
2. Rem Koolhaas, 'De wereld is rijp voor de architect als visionair', *Archis* no. 8, 1986, pp. 45-47.

to Bigness, loses its autonomy and its scale. The individual does not relate to the 'too much' or to the 'oversized' in the same way as to an object or to a system in which it has a clearly defined place: the individual is simultaneously negated and integrated by the massive. The 'too much' and the 'oversized' are Big. Bigness is, however, not the same as colossal. Colossal is yet another object, so it is still relational. Bigness, on the other hand, is so big that the 'inside' detaches itself from its envelope and intrinsically has no more connection with 'outside', becoming an environment in its own right. It creates no image; it creates no place. The individual does not 'count' in the face of Bigness and is no longer a benchmark. Everything that humankind has made in his own image and own scale thus loses its validity here: 'composition, tradition, transparency, ethics', in short, the *city*. Theoretically, however, Koolhaas defines Bigness most tellingly and succinctly in experiential terms, as 'massive presence'. It is a 'too much' that imposes itself.

Bigness is the result of the untrammelled growth of mass production. Growth generates an 'excess': too many people, interrelationships, words, happenings, products, money. However, Koolhaas does not conceive 'mass' as an historic or social phenomenon. He defines it neither from the perspective of social circles and communality nor from the loss of identity through globalisation, nor from the perspective of the 'loss' of clarity in the flood of communication, nor from the perspective of the historic experience of the shift from the qualitative to the quantitative. He does not thematise the tension between the weighty and the light, between the gravity of the archaic or the pre-modern and the unbearable lightness of the hyper-modern. Koolhaas is not a cultural philosopher but a theoretician: he conceives mass as a state of being. Mass is more primordial or more essential than any concrete and limited social or architectural form. There is massiveness underlying any form, as there is chaos behind order or molecules that constitute an organism. The forms extricate themselves from a *potentiality*. In the primitive state of matter of 'mass', the social does not exist as a context or as an association, but is fluid, formless, structureless, and thus also 'freer'. The social therefore becomes 'formless', to use the terms of the Maaskant speech. Moreover, considering taste is a mechanism that reproduces social structures and places, then the formless mass is automatically 'tasteless' as well. In this ontology, every finality is superficial and every Utopia objectively naive. Koolhaas does not regard the traditional communality of the family, the village and the political community of the city – which the history of architecture has long accepted as 'normal' – either as the upholders of values or as the stepping-stones which might lead to a future Metropolis of Mankind. The crisis of the Grand Narratives is, however, no reason to grieve. What might come across as a great loss and a form of cynicism from a humanistic standpoint, as the abandonment of politics and society as an ethical project, is, from this standpoint, a form of lucidity. In historic developments such as neo-urbanism and the explosive growth of those new Asian super-cities, or the chaos which, in Japan, has already become 'an object for consumption' and the 'leitmotif of architecture and urbanism',[3] Koolhaas sees a 'truth' – an ontological principle that is 'breaking through' in history.

Koolhaas wants to think *beyond* the current crisis of traditional social and societal forms. Nevertheless, this crisis shares some intriguing similarities with the crisis of the city-states in Ancient Greece. At the point when the more or less manageable, self-governing community of the *polis,* which provided the framework for the political and moral philosophy of Plato and Aristotle and which also forms the foundation of Western political thinking, had to step aside for more 'global' and also

3. Rem Koolhaas, *Parenthesis,* in 'The End of the Age of Innocence?', J. Lucan, *OMA/Rem Koolhaas,* New York 1991, p. 164.

less stable power structures, there were new philosophical ideas developing that took account of this reality – in the first instance, the materialistic ontology of atomism. This posits that everything which exists and happens is a configuration and movement of a 'mass' of elementary particles. The bodies and figures formed are not enduring and nor do they have an ultimate meaning, since an unending process of transformation re-dissolves all forms in time. The individual therefore must live without the 'horizon' of a framework that is essential or true, and without any expectation of a future redeeming form that will be definitive and meaningful. Society thus has no goal or direction. The complement of this ontology is a new ethic. In a society where the small 'communities' barely have a right to decide, and these communities dissolve in a mass of isolated individuals, then political ideals or engagement no longer make any sense. The ethical-political question – 'Where do *we* want to go?' – therefore remains moot, and politics becomes a case of power and management. Social rules and values will of course always be needed. However, besides this ethic, which has been reduced to an elementary and duty-bound doctrine with the intention of making society 'turn' while it must also guarantee the 'workability' of coexistence, there is still the apolitical question of happiness. When has a life 'succeeded'? When has someone fulfilled his or her potential? For the epicurists and, in another sense, for the stoics as well, morality – *for everyone* – was an individual affair: how could one live worthily in a reality which, taken as a whole, is amoral and ultimately meaningless? The formulation of this question used by classical thinkers on morality under the prevailing political circumstances was 'How does one live worthily in the midst of the masses?' In the midst of 'massive presence'? How to build architecture *for everyone* when one no longer believes in the socio-political utopian ideals, when one goes *beyond* politics?

Koolhaas's view of reality approximates that of classical atomism. The objective condition in which people live (and build) = void + mass. 'Where there is nothing, everything is possible.'[4] Experience does not reveal the essence of things, and it does not give any indication of the ultimate goal, being instead an epiphenomenon. Action is the organisation of homogeneous matter, social reality exists as 'appearance', the 'void' is the principle of movement and transformation, events are the effect of condensation, dying is disappearance, dissolving in homogeneity. A society is composed of chance and temporary configurations, which people cannot control or steer. One can merely create the conditioning framework for society to function. This provides the context for the vast majority of OMA's projects that concern civic or public buildings. Koolhaas's 'public' architecture is not 'political': it is not aimed at the creation of enduring forms of significance, meaning, and it does not fit as a monument in an Image of communality. The perspective on perfection and the detail's claim to eternity are pathetic. Public buildings are structures with a limited lifespan which are only intent on intensity or intensification of the experience. They are flow controls that regulate the densification and acceleration of 'mass'. On top of this – as an unprompted encore – Koolhaas contrasts this intensified activity with voids in the building that 'open up' the experience and where the glance can always escape. Moreover, he nods – for anyone who is interested – to the sparks of meaningless beauty which are the by-product of everything that happens within and with a building: the play of light and colour...

Koolhaas publicly formulates his theory and his conception of reality, but he keeps their complement, his ethic, secret. His ethic comes close to the classical philosophical wisdom that coincided with the disappear-

---

4. Rem Koolhaas, 'Imagining the Nothingness' (1985), in: *S,M,L,XL*, New York/Rotterdam 1995, p. 199.

ance of the *polis,* the city-state, but it is more Roman than Greek. Rome has always been important to Koolhaas, but the reference becomes more and more explicit. Rome is the antique prefiguration of the globalised world as Koolhaas presents it in his analyses and texts. Rome is a chaotic stacking and intermingling that is pragmatically controlled and channelled, self-perpetuating and expansive, yet it is not 'going somewhere'. In the Roman Empire, politics was indeed no longer an ethical project, but concerned the organisation and control of mass in a city-state and in a 'globalised' empire. This – Rome's only true contribution to philosophy – is where atomism evolved further and where the late-classical moral teachings were formulated. The Roman answer to the question of how to live worthily in the midst of this antique Bigness is a concoction of epicurism and stoicism, of ataraxia and autarky, of self-involvement and self-possession, the cultivation of distance, friendship, and the 'inner life'. In order to live worthily, one must – in the words of Baudelaire – learn from being 'alone in the midst of the crowd'. The first and most important means for achieving this is the house or, for those who can afford it, a country house or 'villa'. That is why Koolhaas's crucial references are not merely the ancient metropolis of Rome, but also its complement: the Roman house. Pompeii.

The houses and villas designed by OMA are not numerous, but they are surely crucial. They figure prominently in the many presentations and overviews of the office's output, but Koolhaas says almost nothing about them. The 'discourse' is about public architecture, about the way in which urban planning and architecture function socially, about the position of the designer, and the design process as an intellectual, creative and social practice. *S,M,L,XL,* for example, devotes 120 pages to the two patio villas, the Nexus World housing project in Japan and the Villa Dall'Ava, reassuringly accompanied by warm anecdotes. Yet throughout the entire book there is barely any statement to be found about what a house actually is, or about what should or can happen there. In the 'Dictionary' there is no entry for house, villa or dwelling. One could, of course, argue that the houses which Koolhaas highlights repeatedly in his publications speak for themselves.

For Koolhaas, a house is a place to 'live in secret'. A house can turn away, stand aloof, disengage from its surroundings or from the city in many different ways. Many pre-modern houses form a closed entity, and disengage from their surroundings because they are built around a 'centre' (fire, chimney, staircase, roof...) which symbolically intertwines all the dimensions of life and thus turns the house itself into a 'microcosmos'. The modern middle-class house sooner tends to follow a social logic: it conceals itself behind its facade, it cultivates the interior, guards the entrance and keeps an eye on the street. Koolhaas, however, builds houses which are inward-looking in a 'Roman' way: turned away from their immediate surroundings, organised around the openness of the atrium and *impluvium,* directed towards a 'profane' centre where life comes to a still point. Koolhaas's two patio villas and the 'House in the Forest' take this logic the furthest. The square patio villas (1984-1988) have a half-sunken storey at street level, with the entrance and stairwell, as well as a bedroom and a garage. The staircase climbs to the middle of the upper storey beside an open patio, around which all the rooms are arranged, so there is no entrance to dictate the orientation of the space. Both houses have a spacious and attractive view to the garden – nearly all the published photos look towards to the garden. However, the middle of the house seems to have a stronger draw than the view. The patio is transparent longitudinally, and this keeps the space open, but the transparency itself is not the key. One of the two transverse patio walls is a wall of corrugated metal, almost fully closed. The patio floor is of ground glass and draws light to the storey below during the day. The floor, the glass walls and the metal wall not only reflect the sky and the

light, but at night, when the floor is illuminated from below, they trans-
form the patio into an empty lantern. In publications, the patio is called
the 'empty heart' of the house. This means of turning the house medita-
tively inward is radicalised in the 'House in the Forest' (1992-1994), also
known as the 'Dutch House'. This detached house with guest quarters is
set in the midst of a densely wooded area in the Netherlands. The main
building repeats in broad outline the plan of the patio villas. It is a floating, slab-like oblong with glass walls, with at the 'zero level' – beneath
the 'atrium' on the ground-level storey – a utility space and the entrance.
Because of its isolated setting, this oblong house, unlike the patio villas,
offers an all-round view. However, here the 'empty heart' is enclosed.
The staircase comes out in the middle of the living spaces, but in such a
fashion that the hatch of the trapdoor, which swings open on entering,
seals off and hides the only access to the 'centre'. It is only when one shuts
the trapdoor again – thus closing off the entrance – that one notices the
narrow corridor which leads across the trapdoor, now functioning as a
little drawbridge, to the secret 'middle' of the house: a bedroom and a
bathroom, both opening onto a small inner patio with plain, closed walls.
This means that there is no access from the living space, not even any
visual contact with the private heart of the house. The inner space, where
one is alone with oneself and one's body, is therefore not just isolated
but also hidden. It is a radical choice: here in the middle of the forest,
the most intimate spaces are completely cut off from the 'view' and the
openness round about. The bedroom looks out onto the closed wall of
the small, enclosed patio and a strip of sky. The four walls of the living
spaces do not follow modernist principles either: the glass walls are not
intended to wholly open up the house, nor to assure transparency
between interior and exterior. These walls are made of a variety of reflec-
tive and coloured types of glass, and they can be screened off in various
ways. The resulting effect is that the glass walls are not completely trans-

parent, but function as screens on which the view is refracted and pro-
jected as semi-artificial landscapes – almost in the same way as the closed
inner walls in Roman houses were decorated with landscape frescoes.
The 'House in the Forest' thus recapitulates but radicalises the logic of
the patio villas. It would be difficult to lead a more 'secret life'. The house
has been discussed on a couple of occasions in OMA's publications, but,
just one instance excepted, without revealing the 'heart': the photographer usually goes no further than offering a tempting glimpse into the
corridor that leads to the secret of the house.

The OMA house is not a symbolic centre that encapsulates the world;
it offers no view of the world or yonder, and it is not a 'headquarters' in
the global network. It is an aside and a place of retirement – away from
the 'massive presence'. Like the Roman villa, OMA houses are a 'solution'
for the privileged few, due to the expense and the lack of space for building in the countryside. However, from the Nexus World housing project
in Fukuoka we learn that this residential logic can be translated into a
different typology. The project comprises two blocks of 24 units, almost
square and both three storeys high. The blocks stand on a light and open
plinth which supports a rusticated, dark surrounding wall. The high wall,
almost completely closed, resembles a fortification. Almost all the published photos of the project look down from above, over the wall and
through glass walls into all the apartments simultaneously. In reality,
however, the units are not socially or visually related to one another, and
they do not form an integrated entity, a neighbourhood, or suggest any
conviviality. The interior of each unit is organised around a private inner
court, the interior spaces are open-plan and have plenty of light, but they
only offer a view of blank walls and, looking diagonally upward under a
roof that is raised on one side, a view to the sky. All the units are orient-
ed in the same direction, so they do not face each other but all look out
in rank, across the plain rooftops of the next row of apartments to an

abstract empty sky. They have no view; they do not look out on the 'world'. In a different manner, in this case organised vertically, the complex thus realises the living concept of the villas. The space of the dwelling is interpreted as a secluded place where someone can be alone with him- or herself and a little piece of uninhabitable emptiness or sky, rather than as an element of the city.

Koolhaas's theory and analyses do not encompass what he actually does. The few houses that OMA has built demonstrate a highly reasoned and radical view of what living is or can be. The 'ancient' philosophy that motivates this is the complement – not Utopian, but still highly critical – of the concept of Bigness and massiveness as a basic condition of architecture and urbanism, and as the obligatory starting-point for design. Koolhaas remains as discrete about the significance of his houses as the houses themselves are discrete about the lives that they accommodate. Some things only work if one does not express them explicitly. The theoretical analyses of Koolhaas do not need a 'discourse', whether strategic or intellectual, about living. However, in order to gain a thorough understanding of *Project X,* it is what the discourse does *not* say that seems essential.

Berlin is a laboratory. Its historical richness resides in the prototypical sequence of its models: neoclassical city, early metropolis, modernist testbed, war victim, Lazarus, Cold War demonstration, etc. First bombed, then divided, Berlin is now centerless, a collection of centers, some of which are voids.'[1] This portrait of Berlin, which Rem Koolhaas drew from his collection of metropolitan picture postcards, and from his own urban imagination, catalogues a panorama of historical stations, presenting Berlin as an archaeological site upon which enigmatic circumstances have layered themselves. As a modern-day Pompeii, this city, divided in two by a wall that, at the same time, separated the world into ideological camps, has secured its place next to New York, Paris, and Los Angeles within Koolhaas's manifestos of 'metropolitan architecture'. The characteristic mixture of mass and void, history and destruction, the coexistence of historical form and radically altered reality exists nowhere else as it does in Berlin. The spectrum of contradictions accumulated here has had an especially stimulating effect on OMA's sense of experimentation and peculiar urban optimism: the islandlike situation of West Berlin seemed to provoke questions of identity around the artificial organism of the metropolis in a wholly unique way.

OMA's place of origin is not New York, as one might assume, but Berlin. From there the path led to Manhattan, and thus, ahead the *Delirious New York* of 1978, a book through which Koolhaas became widely known,[2] a less spectacular but similarly 'delirious' Berlin is to be located. Like a red thread, this Berlin winds throughout the early projects and bears silent witness to the past of the Office of Metropolitan Architecture, whose history – how could it be otherwise in this city? – started directly at the Berlin Wall. The paradoxes and aporias in the sandy soil of the Mark Brandenburg represented a mode of perceiving reality that trained the eye well for the psychological terrain of the metropolis and it's 'delirium'. In this place, the hunger for reality could find abundant, exotic nourishment and the desire for contradiction could discover sudden surfaces of friction to lay bare the secret poetic content of this reality.

1. Rem Koolhaas, 'Berlin', *Zone* 1-2 (1986): 4499. See also Rem Koolhaas, 'Urbanisme: Imaginer le néant', *L'architecture d'Aujourd'hui* 238, April 1985, p. 38.
2. Rem Koolhaas, *Delirious New York,* New York 1978.

The User's Guide to AMO

Bruce Sterling

Why would an architecture office, OMA, create a mirror-image office, AMO, 'dedicated to the virtual'? There are a number of practical answers here. First, there is simply less and less distinction to be made between those two realms of practice: physical buildings (commonly designed on computer screens these days), and information, which floods the planet, and cries out for shelter and disciplined organisation. Rem Koolhaas, who is OMA's principal, also teaches at Harvard. AMO, his bi-continental 'think tank', must be quite a handy way to repurpose some of those brighter graduate students.

And then there's the convenience of intellectual habit. Since his own student days in the 1960s, Koolhaas has consistently intermingled architecture and media. He is leading by example here. Rem Koolhaas was once a newspaper reporter. He also wrote big, door-stopping, lavishly illustrated books. He even put himself through architecture school by creating movie scripts. Thus AMO, an outfit whose interests are virtual and informational, but within the context of real physical structures.

The OMA/AMO dichotomy attaches two clickable icons onto a singular process. Trends have favoured this approach, and those dual enterprises have converged within today's highly mediated cities. Blatant examples tower and sprawl on the planet's urban landscape. Libraries are a special Koolhaas interest: they're giant information barns. He's worked on a Chinese broadcasting centre and a German media campus. These are structures whose direct purpose is to make information flow in bulk: the actual building is a node, an information filter, a virtual factory. But all modern buildings share this trend, no matter how distant they may seem from an information economy. Cities are crammed with mobile cell phones and laptops, plug-in PCs, embedded chips and security systems, signals and signage. The digitised metropolis is information-rich, but it's a haphazard, ill-designed business. Poor information architecture has serious consequences: in an urban context it means endless traffic jams, nuisance security, screaming billboards, bewildered taxi drivers, marooned tourists, iffy phone coverage, network outages, utility failures and energy wastage.

Deftly combining skills in the virtual and actual can prove useful indeed when constructing, say, giant train stations in Lille. A massive urban train station like the Lille project, although it's not usually considered 'virtual', is a glaring example of architecture utterly at the mercy of information. A train station is a huge place where no one lives and few ever sleep, a nexus of arrivals, departures, announcements, schedules and timetables, a network node at the core of a city that is a blizzard of numbers, tickets and signs. Subtract the station's information, cut its network links, and nothing can happen there; the builder's walls and rails might still stand, but everything else ceases to be.

A virtual office allows one to think and work outside the standard architectural boxes. Let's briefly consider the justly-famed book *S,M,L,XL,* a self-described Koolhaas 'novel' which concerns itself with ever-vaster scales of urban architecture. I happen to be a science fiction novelist. I confess that I wondered why any architect would ever see fit to design a 'novel', but a syncretic approach can yield some remarkable benefits. I was thrilled to see that *S,M,L,XL* often cites science fiction. This architecture book is certainly far more knowledgeable about science fiction than most science fiction writers ever are about major European architects.

For a 'novel', *S,M,L,XL* boasts a remarkable surplus of essays, manifestos, and big, detailed architectural blueprints. However, it doesn't lack for exciting plot tension and colourful, revelatory characters. Here, on page 1204, the irrepressible Madelon Vriesendorp observes a glittering party crammed with contemporary architects:

And then they started dancing, which was terrible because they were all so frustrated that they had to sort of stamp their feet – like architects. They're so stylized they can't let go, and when they do it's so awful, like a geometric Spanish Dance! It was a horrible party, everybody just hating each other. One had just won a competition and the others were all so envious (and all their first wives were now the others' second wives – like the Dutch government – all the same people just changing places). You could feel the tension. Suddenly we heard a big smash and Richard Rogers had 'thumped' somebody – he had thumped him on the face, and all the blood was running onto these white tiles. A real fight! And everybody pretended that nothing happened. They kept on dancing on the broken glass.

I loved that so much. That kept me turning pages, I can promise you. It explains a remarkable cultural situation so thoroughly that enlightenment dawns in short order.

AMO is a child of the 1990s, but the true origin of AMO probably dates back to the legendary Koolhaas encounter with the Berlin Wall, in 1971.

Now that the Berlin Wall has been conclusively annihilated, this 1971 encounter can properly be seen as a seminal moment in the architectural-virtual. The young Koolhaas (a puckish, paradoxical 1968-er at heart) decides to leave his London architecture school to traipse over to the Berlin Wall, and to write a clever class paper about it. There is something of the whimsical '60s 'put-on' about this notion of a student architecture critique for a Communist military installation. But then Rem Koolhaas actually *encounters the Berlin Wall*. It is sitting there in all its monstrous, gruesomely practical, Cold War physical reality – a vast, totalising, lethal colossus, an endless concrete prison-ramp. A great world city slashed right in two, 'like a brain severed by an artificial scalpel'. No amount of attitudinal posturing is going to save this architecture student from the shattering insights that he gains here.

And what is the single most visible thing about the Berlin Wall (seen from the side of the Free World)? What is the most colourful, most attention-grabbing part of this vast, grim, weirdly beautiful, lethal, massive imposition on the flesh of German civic society? It is graffiti. Endless street-level spray bombings, signs of protest, wisecracks. It is media, it is communication at its most basic and least-policed, a kind of samizdat physically splashed on a vast, brutal structure that benefits no one. This inert tonnage of concrete, barbed wire and steel is one solid, gigantic symbol.

You can travel to modern Berlin today, and you can see that the Berlin Wall, once this implacable byword for the physically unbudge-able, has been virtualised. The Wall is not forgotten, but it has been rendered ghostly. The Berlin Wall is a literal flattered stripe in the streets of the reunited German capital, a kind of timid graphic memento, where mildly disappointed tourists can reminisce over the machine-gun fire and the escape tunnels. That's ironic, of course. But it also makes it dead obvious that a transition from the actual to the virtual is not a weak and genteel business. People can do it in crowds with sledgehammers; they can do it with bulldozers.

Koolhaas has since claimed that this Berlin encounter made him a 'serious student of architecture'. Since achieving that seriousness, he has become especially knowledgeable about the kinds of architecture that do not even pretend to serve humane interests. Wherever cities are delirious, seething with sudden exponential change, or violently mutating into previously unknown forms, Koolhaas is there with camera and notebook. 'Savage' and 'brutal' are words of high praise in the Koolhaas critical vocabulary, for this is a theorist from the dizziest reaches of the ivory tower who never flinches from the brutal, savage truth on the ground.

Like most Dutch people, he may be remarkably soft-spoken about it, but one can't read his work, or even look at his blueprints, without realising that this is a guy who can gaze right through the marquee signs into some kind of mind-boggling heart of darkness. Never one to hide behind the phoney sobrieties of a dirigiste five-year-plan, Koolhaas will jet right over to study the seething, omnivorous urban 'design' of Lagos, Nigeria – and not just any part of Lagos, either, but the densely settled *dump* in Lagos, a planetary nadir of spatial organisation.

As a workaday novelist, ever alert for ironic juxtaposition, I'm really pleased at the image of a Pritzker-Prize-winning architect soberly studying dumps in Lagos. But Koolhaas's incessant planetary travels are not for the photo-ops. Koolhaas further grasps that the Lagos dump is not a 'place' but a process. It's rather like a train station in some ways, for it is a large urban area that is formless (a junk heap), fluid (trash is thrown in and retrieved all the time) and profoundly in transition (for it happens to be on fire). Queasier critics might not grasp the cogent lessons that a dump offers for civic understanding, but it's got plenty.

Confronted with such alarming, trashy formlessness, the natural reaction of Architecture with a capital A is to insist on the eternal proprieties of form-giving. (Thus those Vriesendorp remarks about the fist-fights and the difficulties of dancing.) Perhaps the discriminating, rational mind, ignoring the broken glass underfoot at the banquet, can save itself through classical values. Perhaps some Vitruvian architecture dating to the Roman Empire: something cool, clean, time-honoured, Platonically abstracted. AMO (or rather its civilian wing, the Harvard-based *Project on the City*), demolishes this illusion in the book *Mutations*. Here we find classical Roman urban dynamics recast as a computer game, the 'Roman Operating System'.

The classical Romans were entirely unable to use a modern term like 'operating system', but when AMO lays out the consequences of their everyday urban operations, it is perfectly clear that the Romans, in fact, had one. The Roman Empire was a network-based process in which Roman cities were nodes. 'All Roads Lead to Rome', and that truism is not some kind of charming coincidence, it is the very nature of an imperial structure in which resources, populations, political gossip, the Latin language and the patriotic cults of Mars and Jupiter all moved on roads, which is to say, a standardised, stone-paved, transportation infrastructure. Roman aqueducts are just the same, only more so. New Roman cities get founded on a crossing of Roman roads; stout Roman walls go up to control the flow in and out of the urban precincts. The core of a Roman town is dominated by standardised, highly symbolic structures: the piously appropriate Roman temple, the boasting and strutting Roman victory arches, the giant outdoor Roman amphitheatre where the whole Roman populace can come enjoy the Roman games (generally brought to you by various prominent Roman sponsors).

The lesson to be gained here is that although architecture is a valuable skill-set – it's hard work to build a Roman temple that doesn't fall right down – no temple ever stands without steady flows through those roads and gates. The glorious temple may have a form built in a slavish adherence to the proportions of the Golden Mean, but if the operating system crashes, you're left with an inert, slowly crumbling marble box. No road, no Roman Empire. This being understood, one can take a further useful step. Don't design an impressive showpiece for the ages, and then jam some operations inside of it. Try to grasp the inherent nature of the operations, and then design the structure to shelter them. And if this means, in a modern context, that buildings should not be rigidly built to outlast the next two millennia, but are rather 'stalls', sheds, Prada storefront windows even… Why not go for that?

Bolstered by this insight, one might go further yet. One might daringly embrace the Koolhaas fondness for 'voids' and simply *remove* big chunks of architecture. Like, say, at Euralille train station, where a highway, a railway, three levels of parking, and a metro, all converge on a large, central… emptiness. But of course, this 'void', this 'Piranesian space' in the train station is not a featureless vacuity. It is healthy air and sunlight, a revelatory urban openness. It is not a 'nothingness', but a letting-go, a blissful absence of architecture.

Taking the opposite tack can have a similarly provocative effect. The modern European Union is a European Operating System that has succeeded and considerably outdone the Roman Empire. But it has, in the insightful words of AMO, an 'iconographic deficit'. Why? Because 'Europe', unlike Caesar's Rome, is a soft-power empire. Over decades, 'Europe' has proceeded quite stealthily, avoiding military clashes while working slowly and Eurocratically on the scarcely-visible standards of all those aqueducts and viaducts. And, not coincidentally, 'Europe' is also closely regulating the size, shape and manufacturing specs of (among other products) footwear, fertilizer, smokestacks, livestock, trademarks, cosmetics, pressure vessels, and of course international railroads.

And lo and behold, if one mindfully changes these subtle flows, it

turns out that the whole structure of European society gently changes
in tandem. It proves unnecessary to mount gigantic, rigid Albert Speer
architectural spectacles, and then go put everybody else to the sword in
a totalitarian quest for ruthless dominance. Europe can be unified
through process: by the cheery fact that one can get off a train without
a passport, follow the language-free, international signage, and have a
tasty Tuborg beer in Athens, paid for with the Euros you got in Valencia.

But wait, there's more! If one is an angry barbarian Goth or Vandal
anxious to combat this imperial European Union, there turns out to be
very little there to vandalise. There's a strange Koolhaasian void in the
symbolic centre of Europe. There's very little on strutting Roman display there, except for the bland-looking, architecturally top-heavy Euro
coinage, and a sadly anonymous plain blue Euro flag with its twelve plain
stars. This dusty emblem is still serving duty, somehow, even though
modern Europe no longer has a mere 12 nations in it, but a whacking
twenty-five. Who is properly equipped to confront a problem of this
scope? AMO is a natural choice. With whispers of encouragement from
European Commissioner Romano Prodi and Belgian prime minister Guy
Verhofstadt, AMO supplies Europe with a new 'image-bite'. The result-
ant 'BarCode Flag' for Europe is not, in point of fact, flying over all
Europe today, but that's probably because it does way too good a job.

'Europe' doesn't actually want to be dragged out of the subtle diplo-
matic background with an image this effective. A wise political decision
perhaps, for any imperial symbol this potent would give those vandals
something to ritually burn and the car-bombers a handsome target to
blow up. Nevertheless, the AMO Barcode Flag for Europe is a well-nigh
perfect representation for an all-absorbent, twenty-first century, multi-
national political entity. It is an unprecedented flag for an unprecedented political arrangement.

The Barcode Flag is entirely contemporary, for it would be trivially easy to manufacture in bulk today, but utterly impossible to tediously sew and stitch under all previous, primitive, flag-making technical circumstances. For the Barcode is simply all the flags of Europe, with their loudly assertive yet minimally variant colour schemes, splayed with keenly regulated precision across a single playing field. It's a flag that speaks to the way Europe is. The result is very far from visually unified. But then again, neither is Europe. And there would seem to be quite some room to stick on a lot more such barcoding. Given Europe's expansionary ambitions, a feature like this would be handy.

The AMO Barcode Flag really is the best symbol ever created for Europe, even though today's Europeans are barely able to look at it without a flinch, a headshake, and perhaps a bit of nervous laughter. For it is not any simpleminded, singular, national flag: it is savage, complex, sophisticated, open-ended, garish, wild, and brutally jammed together. At first glimpse, it may seem like a clever prank. And yet, given time, it can indeed be seen to be beautiful. It is calming, educational, even serene, after a while. Eventually, it feels good. Because it's the truth.

A science fiction writer naturally wonders what comes next for a virtual architecture outfit. AMO serves its clients, and there is obviously room for future development for someone who can construct a showpiece actual building that also smoothly integrates brand identity and an interface for the customer, guest, staffer, and consumer. At the logical horizon of this arc of development, though, are the dangerous shoals of the Smart House, the Smart Building, the Smart City.

Here some deep theoretical rethinking would be very welcome. These smartening enterprises have been conspicuous failures to date. They are geeky, thumb fingered and impractical, because they have been imperial impositions of a clumsy digital operating system onto the primal needs of architectural practice. The purpose of shelters and housing is to shel-

ter and house; there is no innate need to be smart, intelligent or artifi-
cially thoughtful. Few people have ever found comfort in the cybernetic
automation of domestic life, for that is no more pleasing to the architect's client than living in software shrinkwrap. However, no modern
inhabited building can exist without ever-changing systemic flows of
water, fuel, sewage, electrical power, light, warmed air, cooled air, and
data. Urban life could be improved if all these flows were far more closely monitored and adjusted in real-time, not through a magic Artificial
Intelligence that outthinks humanity a la *deus ex machina,* but through
ubiquitous, dependable sensors arranged in well-designed, sturdy, reac-
tive networks.

Today's structures depend on brute force to survive storms and earthquakes. Better buildings would swiftly sense a change in physical circumstances and react in real-time. Strain gauges in bridges and highways
could substitute information for materials, becoming the nervous system of a lighter, cheaper, sleeker world. If sensors and communications
were cheap enough, even lowly bricks might have them, so that brick
walls would report automatically on spreading cracks and crumbling
mortar. After a storm, shingles would formally regret their status as miss-
ing-in-action from the roof.

At this stage of development, any division between virtual and actual
becomes practically meaningless: the architectural-virtual has reached
its apotheosis as the everyday way of life. One no longer need explain
the mirror of AMO and OMA, for it seems odd and archaic that they
were ever separated in the first place. The only wonder left in the enterprise is that anyone should ever feel the need to write about it.

n the Downtown Athletic Club each 'plan' is an abstract composition of activities that describes, on each of the synthetic platforms, a different 'performance' that is only a fragment of the larger spectacle of the Metropolis. ... Such an architecture is an aleatory form of 'planning' life tself: in the fantastic juxtaposition of its activities, each of the Club's floors is a separate instalment of an infinitely unpredictable intrigue that extols the complete surrender to the definitive instability of life in the Metropolis.[1]

When Rem Koolhaas defined the 'Culture of Congestion' in *Delirious New York,* he looked back to look ahead: he exposed the often unconscious strategy of radical hybridity present in the psychological exploration of Surrealism but also in the normative modernism of American mid-century corporate architecture. In his own projects (La Villette, Euralille, Congrexpo, ZKM, Jussieu, etc.) Koolhaas developed, accelerated, and refined the hybrid ethos, breathing life into this strategy through an aggressive urban and architectural research program. The aura that Koolhaas's work legitimately produced has become something altogether different in its contemporary proliferation as a generalised public realm. In its propagation, hybridity has endlessly reproduced the image of a pluralised and invigorated public, but its effects have returned once again to the unconscious, repeating ad nauseum the cross-programming strategies that were once radical but which are now only facile. Such strategies, which only twenty or thirty years ago created new worlds through the alchemy of juxtaposed conclusion, have become familiar in the hands of the less imaginative, and have only produced the repetitive inconclusiveness of hybridity as a technique rather than a proposition. The image of radicality in these derivative projects is not enough to veil their overwhelming nostalgia for a remembrance of radicality recently past.

. Rem Koolhaas, 'Definitive Instability: The Downtown Athletic Club', *Delirious New York,* New York 1978, p. 157

Rem Koolhaas

After having lived in Indonesia between 1952 and 1956, Rem Koolhaas (born in 1944) settled in Amsterdam as a journalist for the *Haagse Post* and as a film screenplay writer, before leaving for London to study architecture at the Architectural Association School. Two theoretical projects come from this period: *The Berlin Wall as Architecture* (1970) and *Exodus or the Voluntary Prisoners of Architecture* (1972).

A scholarship obtained in 1972 allowed Koolhaas to stay in the United States. He studied at Cornell University, and then became a Visiting Fellow at the Institute for Architecture and Urban Studies in New York. Fascinated by New York, he started to analyse the impact of metropolitan culture on architecture and published *Delirious New York, a Retroactive Manifesto for Manhattan* (1978).

At this stage, Rem Koolhaas wanted to progress from theory to practical application and decided to return to Europe. In London in 1975, he created, with Elia and Zoe Zenghelis and Madelon Vriesendorp, the Office for Metropolitan Architecture (OMA), whose objectives were the definition of new types of relations – theoretical as well as practical – between architecture and the contemporary cultural situation. In 1978, several commissions in Holland led him to open an agency in Rotterdam which was to henceforth centralise OMA's activities. At the same time, he created the Groszstadt Foundation, an independent structure controlling the cultural activities of the agency, such as exhibitions and publications.

In 1995, Rem Koolhaas, together with graphic designer Bruce Mau, produced *S,M,L,XL* a book on contemporary society, building and urban development, also documenting the work of OMA.

Since 1995 Rem Koolhaas is professor at Harvard University. He leads a series of research projects for the Harvard *Project on the City,* a student-based research group, founded at Harvard to study different issues affecting the urban condition. The projects include a study of five cities in the Chinese Pearl River Delta, 'Shopping', an analysis of the role of retail consumption in the contemporary city and a study of Lagos, Nigeria. In 2000 two of these research projects were published: *The Great Leap Forward* and *A Guide to Shopping.*

Rem Koolhaas has received, among others, the Rotterdam Maaskant Prize (1986), L'équerre d'argent for Maison à Bordeaux, the Antonio Gaudi Prize for the Lille Urbanism Project (1992), the Pritzker Architecture Prize (2000) and the Praemium Imperiale Award (2003).

OMA

OMA was founded with the ambition to address contemporary society and to build contemporary architecture. Early work consists of a number of polemic competition entries. In 1978 a competition entry for the extension of the Dutch Parliament won first prize ex aequo. Appreciation for this design resulted in the first major commissions, both in the Netherlands: the master plan for a housing quarter in Amsterdam, completed in 1986, and the Netherlands Dance Theatre in The Hague, completed in 1987.

In the 1980s and '90s OMA entered a series of major competitions, in 1982 Parc de La Villette, in 1989 the Très Grande Bibliothèque and in 1993 the library of Jussieu, all in Paris. In this period, the office realised several projects, ranging from private residences to large scale urban planning. In 1991, the Villa dall'Ava overlooking the Eiffel Tower and Nexus Housing and two apartment-blocks in Fukuoka, Japan, were completed. In 1992 the Kunsthal and its Museum Park in Rotterdam were opened. And in 1994, OMA planned Euralille, a business and civic centre hosting the major high-speed train hub in the north of France.

Although most realised projects were built in the Netherlands and in France, the office took a special interest in Asia which resolved in the foundation of a Hong Kong based branch: OMA Asia.

At the start of the new century the office is active in the U.S. with a series of Prada stores in New York, San Francisco and Los Angeles; the new Seattle Public Library and the McCormick Tribune Campus Center at the IIT University of Chicago. In all these projects OMA is also consultant in redefining the corporate identity of the client organisation in the context of its architectural planning. In the planning process concerning the possible relocation of the Netherlands' main airport to an island in the North Sea, OMA was asked to consider what positive impact such an operation could have on the identity of the Netherlands.

OMA's main activities in Europe at this moment are a new concert hall for Porto, Portugal, the construction of a new city centre in Almere, the Netherlands, and the new Dutch Embassy in Berlin, Germany.

Currently OMA is engaged in its largest project ever: the new headquarters for the Central Chinese Television (CCTV), a 550.000 m² headquarter and cultural centre in Beijing, to be completed in 2008 for the Olympic Games.

OMA employs almost 100 architects and designers of multi-national origin. A constant change of staff is considered a valuable source of new input and expertise. Continuity is guaranteed by a select group of project leaders with a long-term commitment to the firm and a special affinity with their projects. Architects, designers, CAD-architects, model makers and graphic designers work in close collaboration. Expert consultants on relevant issues are involved from the beginning of the design process. During construction, locally based teams, combining local and Rotterdam staff, work on site. At present, OMA is generally considered one of the leading architecture firms in the world.

AMO

Somewhere in the late 1990s, while working on the design for the new headquarters for Universal (currently Vivendi), OMA was first exposed to the full pace of change that engulfed the world of media and with it the increasing importance of the virtual domain.

This led Rem Koolhaas and OMA to create a new company, AMO, exclusively dedicated to the investigation and perform-ance in this realm. While OMA remains dedicated to the rea-lisation of architectural projects, AMO applies architectural thinking in its pure form to questions of organisation, identity, culture and program, and defines ways – from the conceptual to the operative – to address the full potential of the contem-porary condition. AMO embodies both the professional expe-rience of OMA and knowledge generated by the Harvard Design School *Project on the City*.

AMO often works parallel to OMA for the same clients, pro-viding extra services in the domains of organisation and iden-tity while, at the same time, work on the design of a building is being conducted. This is, for instance, the case for PRADA: while OMA worked on the design of three shops (New York, San Francisco and Los Angeles), AMO worked on PRADA's in store information technology, the website and media con-tent. This also led to work on PRADA's advertising campaigns and general business consulting. Since its conception, AMO also acts as a consultant for WIRED –a magazine on the impact of technological inventions on contemporary society. Most recently AMO has been involved in a brainstorm on the visual communication of Europe organised by the European Commission.

Bibliography

Content, by OMA-AMO/Rem Koolhaas/&&&, edited by Brendan McGetrick, Köln 2003
Harvard Design School Guide to Shopping, Köln 2001
Harvard Design School Great Leap Forward, Köln 2001
OMA/AMO Rem Koolhaas Projects for Prada Part 1, Milan 2001
OMA: S,M,L,XL together with the Canadian graphic designer Bruce Mau, Rotterdam/New York 1995
Delirious New York: A Retroactive Manifesto for Manhattan, New York 1978. Reprinted in 1994 by 010 Publishers, Rotterdam. Translated into German, Japanese, French and Italian. Portuguese and Spanish soon to follow.

Selected Publications

Kenchiku Bunka, February 2003
A+Universal, January 2001
New York Times Magazine, July 9th, 2000
Wired Magazine, June 2000
OMA@work.a+u, special edition, March 2000
Time Magazine, December 21, 1998
Kenchiku Bunka, Vol. 54 no. 628, February 1999
Architecture and Urbanism no.217, October 1988
Arch+, no.132, June 1996
Kenchiku Bunka, Vol. 50 no. 579, January 1995
El Croquis no.53, March 1992 and no.79, 1996
L'Architecture d'Aujourd'hui, no.280, April 1992
Lucan, Jacques, *OMA/Rem Koolhaas,* New York 1991
Goulet, Patrice, *Six Projets,* Paris 1990
Goulet, Patrice, *Lille,* Paris 1990
Architecture d'Aujourd'hui, no.238, April 1985

1972

Exodus, or the Voluntary Prisoners of Architecture
Final project at the Architectural Association School of
Architecture, London
Entry for *Casabella's* 'The City as meaningful Environment',
first prize ex aequo

1976

The Story of the Pool
New York, USA

1978

**Delirious New York: A Retroactive Manifesto for
Manhattan**
Book by Rem Koolhaas. Oxford University Press, reprinted by
010 Publishers in 1994, translated into German, French and
Japanese

1984

Netherlands Dance Theater, Project II
The Hague, the Netherlands
Completed 1987
Performance and rehearsal facilities for Dutch modern dance
company

1984

Villa Dall'Ava
St. Cloud, Paris, France
Completed 1991
'Glass house' for a family of three, rooftop pool with
view of Eiffel Tower
Prix d'Architecture du Moniteur

1987

Kunsthal
Rotterdam, the Netherlands
Completed 1992
Hall for temporary exhibitions with three major exhibition
spaces (7,000 m²)

1988

Euralille: Centre International d'Affaires
Lille, France
Phase I completed 1994, Phase II completion 2005

General master plan, architectural supervision. Le Centre
Euralille by Jean Nouvel-Emmanuel Cattani;
La Gare Lille-Europe by Jean-Marie Duthilleul; World Trade
Center by Claude Vasconi; Tour Crédit Lyonnais by Christian
de Portzamparc; Four-Star Hotel by François and Marie
Delhay; Le parc urbaine by Empreinte; complementary
infrastructure by Antoine Béal and Ludovic Blancaert.
Antonio Gaudi Prize, Olympic Awards, 1992

1989

Sea Terminal
Zeebrugge, Belgium
Competition, first prize
Departure/arrival point for channel ferries with conference
centre, customs, casino and entertainment facilities

1990

Congrexpo (Lille Grand Palais)
Lille, France
Completed 1994
Part of Euralille master plan. Congress center 18,000 m²,
Zenith rock theater 7,850 m², Expo 20,000 m² space divisible
into three equal spaces, Parking with 1,500 enclosed spaces

1992

Educatorium
Utrecht, the Netherlands
Completed 1997
10,000 m² multi-use academic facilities: canteen for 1,000
people, auditoriums for 400 and 500 people and examination
halls (150, 200 and 300 people)

1992

Dutch House
The Netherlands
Completed 1993
Private residence for two permanent residents and three
occasional residents (517 m²).

1993

2 Bibliothèques de Jussieu
Paris, France
Competition, first prize
Library of humanities (8,000 m²), library of science and
research (10,000 m²), reception and public space (1,000 m²),
relogements (3,000 m²) and parking (3,700 m²).

1994

Maison à Bordeaux
France
Completed 1998
Private residence for family of five (500 m²)
Best design of 1998 by *Time Magazine*, L'Equerre d'Argent

1994

Almere Master Plan
Almere, the Netherlands
Completion 2005
Master plan for a new center for the City of Almere, built on
regained land: 1,100 housing units, 4,300 parking spaces,
leisure 9,000 m², theater 8,000 m², pop/concert hall 2,000 m²,
library 8,000 m², art school 7,000 m², extension hospital with
32,000 m² and 600 parking spaces, offices
130,000 m², extension Almere Station, 100-room hotel,
commercial 53,000 m², waterfront of 1 km, and
infrastructure

1995

Universal City
Los Angeles, USA
Study. Master plan and headquarters building

1995

S,M,L,XL
Book
By Rem Koolhaas and Bruce Mau
1346 pages (010 Publishers, Rotterdam and Monacelli
Press, New York)
Book Award of the American Institute of Architects in 1997

1997

IIT
Chicago, USA
Competition, first prize
Completion 2003
Campus centre for the Illinois Institute of Technology
(10,700 m²)

1997

Netherlands Embassy
Berlin, Germany
Completion 2003

Total 8,500 m², 4,800 m² offices, 1,500 m² housing,
2,200 m² parking

1998

Almere Block 6
Almere, the Netherlands
Under construction
Design of multiplex cinema (5,050 m²) and shopping
centre (2,600 m²).

1998

MAB-Tower
Rotterdam, the Netherlands
Tower complex with 40,000 m² offices, 30,000 m² housing,
10,000 m² hotel, 13,000 m² mixed use (commercial) and
7,000 m² parking.

1999

Seattle Public Library
Seattle, USA
Completion 2004
New central library for Seattle (33,000m²)

1999

Casa da Musica
Porto, Portugal
Competition, first prize. Completion 2004
Concert hall, large auditorium with 1,500 seats, small
auditorium with 350 seats, facilities

1999

Prada Epicenter Broadway
New York, USA
Completed 2001
The projects for the Italian fashion company Prada span from
research on shopping and new concepts for Prada as a
brand to the creation of three big stores in the United States.

1999

Prada Epicenter Beverly Hills
Los Angeles, USA
Completion 2004

1999

Prada IT
In-store Technology
A series of experiential and service-oriented features
enhancing both functioning and aura of the stores

2000

Astor Hotel
New York, USA
Study in collaboration with Herzog & DeMeuron

2000

Guggenheim Hermitage
Las Vegas, USA
Completed 2001
A 460 m² gallery, bookstore and gift shop

2000

Guggenheim Las Vegas
Las Vegas, USA
Completed 2001
A 2,800 m² museum accessed via the casino level
of the Venetian Hotel

2000

Brussels, Capital of Europe
Brussels, Belgium
Identity Project

2000

CCC
Cordoba, Spain
Completion 2005
Congress Centre

2000

LACMA
Los Angeles, USA
Completion 2006
LA Country Museum of Art, Los Angeles

2000

New Whitney
New York, USA
Completion 2006

2002

Koningin Julianaplein
The Hague, the Netherlands
Competition

2002

CCTV
Beijing, China
Completion 2008
New headquarters for the China Central Television.
553,000 m², one of the first of 300 towers to be
constructed in Beijing's new Central Business District

Aaron Betsky is an architect, an architecture historian and critic, and the director of the Netherlands Architecture Institute (NAI) in Rotterdam. Between 1995 and 2001, he was curator of architecture, design and digital projects at the San Francisco Museum of Modern Art (SF-MOMA). His publications include *Landscrapers* (Thames and Hudson, 2002), *Architecture Must Burn* (Thames and Hudson, 2000) and *The Houses of Max Palevsky* (Rizzoli, 2002).

Ian Buruma was born in the Netherlands to a Dutch father and English mother. Though educated in both Holland and Japan, Ian Buruma spent a great deal of his life in Asia. He was a fellow at the Woodrow Wilson Institute for the Humanities in Washington and is currently Luce Professor of Human Rights and Journalism at Bard College, New York. He has written such books as *God's Dust: A Modern Asian Journey; Behind the Mask;* and *The Wages of Guilt: Memories of War in Germany and Japan*. His novel, *Playing the Game,* is a fictional biography about the life of an Indian prince who played cricket in Britain. His latest books are *Bad Elements* and *Inventing Japan.*

Okwui Enwezor Artistic Director of Documenta 11 was former Artistic Director of the second Johannesburg Biennale and Adjunct Curator of Contemporary Art at the Art Insitute of Chicago. He is founder and publisher of *Nka: Journal of Contemporary African Art* (Cornell University, Ithaca). Among his many books is *Under Siege: Four African Cities, Freetown, Johannesburg, Kinshasa, Lagos.* He is a Visiting Professor in the Department History of Art and Architecture, University of Pittsburgh.

H.J.A.Hofland writes columns in *NRC Handelsblad* and *De Groene Amsterdammer.* He lived for quite a long time in the United States (Johnstown, Pennsylvania and Manhattan) and has published book-length essays (including *Tegels lichten, De élite verongelukt, Het voorgekookt bestaan),* travelogues (including *De wording van het Wilde Oosten*) and novels (including *De Alibicentrale, Man van zijn eeuw*) and has made television documentaries in association with Hans Keller. (including *Nederland 1938 - 1948, Vastberaden maar soepel en met mate*). In 2001 the Universiteit van Maastricht gave him an honorary doctorate.

Neil Leach is an architect and theorist. He has taught at a number of institutions including the Architectural Association, London, and Columbia University, New York. He is the author of *The Anaesthetics of Architecture* (MIT, 1999), *Millennium Culture* (Ellipsis, 1999), *Camouflage* (forthcoming), *The Politics of Space* (forthcoming) and *Forget Heidegger* (Paideia, forthcoming), co-author of *Marspants* (Architecture Foundation, 2000), editor of *Rethinking Architecture* (Routledge, 1997), *Architecture and Revolution* (Routledge, 1999), *The Hieroglyphics of Space* (Routledge, 2002) and *Designing for a Digital World* (Wiley, 2002); co-editor of *Digital Tectonics* (Wiley, forthcoming), and co-translator of L.B. Alberti, *On the Art of Building in Ten Books* (MIT, 1988).

Matthew Stadler is a novelist and editor who lives in Astoria, Oregon. During a two-years residence in the Netherlands he contributed to the journal *Wiederhall* and presented papers at architecture conferences in Delft and Rotterdam. His 1994 paper, 'I Think I'm Dumb', concerning the American West Coast and Rem Koolhaas's manifesto for 'Bigness', is online at *The Raven Chronicles.* He is the co-founder and editor of *Clear Cut Press* and the literary editor of *Nest Magazine.*

Michael Bruce Sterling is a science fiction author and journalist. His first science fiction story, *Man-Made Self* was published in 1976. Along with William Gibson, John Shirley, and Rudy Rucker, Sterling became in the 1980s one of the most prominent voices of the 'cyberpunk' movement. He wrote and edited at that time a photocopied 'zine' called *Cheap Truth* in which he and a number of collaborators mocked the science fiction establishment and called for a new, more vibrant, and more culturally relevant approach to the genre. Sterling has written numerous books and articles. His most recent ones include *Distraction* (1998) a novel about politics and bioengineering, *A Good Old-Fashioned Future* (1999) a short story collection and *Zeitgeist* (2000) a postmodern fantasy set at the turn of the millennium. His most recent work, *Tomorrow Now: Envisioning the Next 50 Years,* is a non-fiction work of futurist speculation.

Bart Verschaffel is a full professor in the Department of Architecture and Urban Planning Faculty of Ghent University and at the University of Antwerp. He publishes work in the field of art and architecture history and cultural philosophy. His published monographs include: *De Glans der Dingen* (1989), *Figuren/essays* (1995), and *Architecture is (as) a gesture* (2001).

This book accompanies the travelling exhibition on the work of OMA, titled *Content*. The exhibition was organised by OMA and the Staatliche Museen zu Berlin, in cooperation with the Netherlands Architecture Institute. It was first presented at the Neue Nationalgalerie in Berlin (November 15, 2003 - January 18, 2004) and opened at the Kunsthal in Rotterdam in March 2004. The exhibition will travel on in 2004 and 2005 throughout Europe, the United States and Asia.

Special thanks to: Rem Koolhaas and Kayoko Ota for their important suggestions and feedback while working on the concept en structure of the book and to Chantal Defesche and Mariëtte van Stralen at OMA for their generosity and time, guiding us through the incredible collection of visuals on OMA/AMO's work.

Compiled and Edited by
Véronique Patteeuw

Translation
Pierre Bouvier (H.J.A. Hofland; René Boomkens)
Brian Holmes (Jean Attali)
Andrew May (Bart Verschaffel)

English copy-editing
D'Laine Camp

English proofreading
D'Laine Camp

Design
Thonik

Lithography and printing
Drukkerij Die Keure, Bruges

Publisher
Simon Franke

Credits
Peter Aaron/Esto 14t
AMO 22-23, 74-75, 137, 142-143
Chris Dercon cover image
Richard Barnes 138-139
Rem Koolhaas 73, 78-79
Ari Marcopoulos 150-151
Jean-Marie Monthiers 82-83
OMA 16-17, 18-19, 144-145, 150-151
Philippe Ruault 12-13
Hans Werlemann 9, 10-11, 14b, 15, 20, 21, 76-77, 80-81, 84-85, 86-87, 140-141, 146-147, 148-149

Available in North, South and Central America through D.A.P./Distributed Art Publishers Inc., 155 Sixth Avenue 2nd Floor, New York, NY 10013-1507, Tel. 212 6271999, Fax. 212 6279484.

Available in the United Kingdom and Ireland through Art Data, 12 Bell Industrial Estate, 50 Cunnington Street, London W4 5HB, Tel. 0208 7471061, Fax. 0208 7422319.

NAi Publishers is an internationally orientated publisher specialised in developing, producing and distributing books on architecture, the visual arts and related disciplines. www.naipublishers.nl

Printed and bound in Belgium

ISBN 90-556-349-4